Speak Québec!

A Guide to Day-to-Day Quebec French

DANIEL KRAUS

SPEAK QUÉBEC!
A GUIDE TO DAY-TO-DAY QUEBEC FRENCH

iUniverse books may be ordered through booksellers or by contacting:

iUniverse
1663 Liberty Drive
Bloomington, IN 47403
www.iuniverse.com
1-800-Authors (1-800-288-4677)

Because of the dynamic nature of the Internet, any web addresses or links contained in this book may have changed since publication and may no longer be valid. The views expressed in this work are solely those of the author and do not necessarily reflect the views of the publisher, and the publisher hereby disclaims any responsibility for them.

Any people depicted in stock imagery provided by Thinkstock are models, and such images are being used for illustrative purposes only. Certain stock imagery © Thinkstock.

ISBN: 978-1-5320-0250-2 (sc)
ISBN: 978-1-5320-0252-6 (hc)
ISBN: 978-1-5320-0251-9 (e)

Print information available on the last page.

iUniverse rev. date: 12/08/2016

For Mom and Dad…
Who always taught
that the only true boundaries
between cultures are those
we ourselves create.

Thanks

Sincere thanks to the following persons, without whom this book could not have been created:

Michel Besner, Yves Boudreault, la famille Brossart-Galley (Chantal, Jean-François, Anne-Lise et Églantine), Corinne et Francis Prévote, Martin Chouinard, Thérèse Bruno, Claude Cajolet, Michel Collet, Virginia Crabbé, Nancy Daoust, Eva Dawson, François DesRochers, François du Monthier, François Dunn, Nicholas Ericson, Martin Faucher, Paul and Stacey Ford and family, Eric Godin, Claudia Goyette, Amélie Hébert, Jean-Jacques Hermans, Marie-Claude Hudon, Nina Jones, Peter Kreutlein, Jean Lachance, Luc Laprise, Jacques Larue-Langlois, Laurent Lauzon, Sébastien Lavier, Christian Lavoie, Éric Lebel, Lyne Michaud, Sandra LeMieux, Isabelle LeMieux, Caroline Lévesque, Raymond Lévesque et famille, Raya Mileva, Nancy Nadeau, Sammy Nelson, Ann Nickner, François Perusse, Scott Rafer, Manuel Rochon, Michael Sheasby and family, Greg Smith and Diane Laflamme, Michael-David Smith and family, Elisabeth Starenkyj, Steven Tabac, Lisa and Michael Taylor and family, Carol Swedlow, Pierre Toussignant, Josée Tremblay, Marie-Josée Turcotte, Raphael Van Lierop, Keiko Watanabe, Sophie Vincelette and Tami Weinberg.

Special thanks to André Gauthier, Alain Laferrière, Sébastien Lavier, and Nancy Foran, whose corrections, thoughts, and ideas contributed significantly to this work.

Contents

Preface

This fourth edition of *Speak Québec* is truly a milestone. With over five thousand copies in print, what began as a handy list for friends has now grown into a well-known reference to the Québécois language. For some – largely Francophone readers – this book provides an interesting (and often amusing) source of insight into English. For English-speaking readers, this book has proven to be an important tool for understanding and communicating at work and in social situations.

The interest that people have taken in *Speak Québec* has been an enormous factor in its growth and success. Since publishing the first edition in 2000, I've received countless emails and letters from both visitors and residents of Quebec, offering suggestions, insights, encouragement, and thanks. For this, I am deeply grateful.

Through the years spent working on this book, I have grown ever more amazed by the richness and evolution of the Québécois language. While many of the terms and ideas you'll find herein are rooted in Quebec's rural history, the language itself continues to grow with a depth and colour that is a credit to the Québécois culture. The humour and frankness of the Quebecers truly shines through in the pages that follow.

My sincere hope is that this fourth edition, the result of almost fifteen years of work, research, and discussion, continues to open the doors of Quebec culture to visitors, residents, and amateurs of Quebec and her language.

Daniel Kraus
Montreal, Quebec
August 2016

Introduction

Although many works have been published in recent years to help French speakers better understand the many unique words and expressions found in Quebec, almost no such resources exist to help English speakers. As any English Canadian or American visitor to the *province de Québec* will tell you, the dizzying array of words and phrases particular to the region creates an almost insurmountable barrier to communicating in French, even for those with a strong command of vocabulary and grammar.

The daily language heard in Quebec can actually be thought of as a "superset" of International French. Quebecers comfortably use most French words, but they also supplant them with several thousand additional words and colloquialisms of their own. While French speakers worldwide often joke about the great differences between their spoken and written languages, nowhere is this more evident than in Quebec – few of the thousands of differences from International French heard in conversation are ever written down. Quebecers proudly point out that a good percentage of this rich, textured language comes from *le vieux français* (Old French), which was brought by the first settlers. This French is complemented by a number of words adopted both from the Inuit (Canada's northern aboriginal people) and First Nations as well as from modern English. These influences combine to form a language that retains all the expansive and artistic nuances of International French while also being endowed with the rich cultural detail and informality of North-American English.

Speak Québec! is designed to be used by English speakers as a practical handbook for understanding Québécois – the day-to-day French spoken in Quebec. It is also highly valuable for francophones who wish to understand the English equivalents of common colloquialisms. By no means a dictionary of officially recognized "Canadian French," this book is intended to clearly explain the vocabulary and expressions necessary to speak the rich vernacular found in and around the province of Quebec. I deliberately make no judgments as to what is technically or grammatically "correct," seeking instead to provide the real-world picture of the language needed to understand and appreciate the Québécois culture.

The first part of this work provides a brief history of the Québécois language, from its origins in New France and the Amerindian tongues to its modern-day influences from English. It also provides a clear explanation of differences in grammar and pronunciation from International French. The second part of the book is a dictionary, a lexicon containing two thousand of the words and phrases most commonly heard throughout the province and most necessary for understanding.

The fundamental goal of this book is to open the doors for better communication and cultural exchange between the Québécois people and others, both domestic and abroad. I wish you luck as you unlock the nuances of this tremendously rich and varied language, and I hope this work provides a concrete means of grasping the joie de vivre that stands behind one of North America's most unique and undiscovered cultures.

A Brief Linguistic History

New France (?–1763)

The evolution of the Québécois[1] language actually began in prehistory, long before the arrival of the first Europeans. The Inuit, Native Americans who had migrated thousands of years earlier across the frozen expanse of the Bering Strait, developed – unbeknownst to them – many words that survive in daily Québec parlance to this day. The First Nations – such as the Micmac, the Cree, and the Outaouais – also had a hand in developing the modern Québec tongue, as their cultures grew and thrived and as they developed words for the unique world around them.

The arrival of the first French explorer (Jacques Cartier, in 1534) brought French traditions, language, and culture of the period

---

[1] Please note the deliberate use of both Québécois/Québec and Quebecer/Quebec. This distinction is deliberate and intentional. Quebecers often differentiate between Québécois (i.e., Quebecers, or residents of Quebec) and "Québécois de souche." The latter designates francophone Quebecers who can trace most or all of their lineage back to the colony of New France. For our purposes, I am using Québécois as a shorthand for Québécois de souche. The French spelling Québec is used when referring specifically to the province's traditional francophone language, culture, history, and/or people. Quebec and Quebecer are used when making more general, perhaps more inclusive, references.

1

to Quebec. Although Cartier made three separate trips to North America – travelling up the St. Lawrence River as far south as Montreal – it was only half a century later, with the founding of Quebec City in 1608 by Samuel de Champlain, that France had a true foothold in the New World. The quickly blossoming fur trade in Quebec brought a rising tide of explorers to the province. With the founding of Ville Marie (modern-day Montreal) in 1642, French presence in the colonies increased quickly, and the development of the province of Quebec was afoot.

Although the language used in Quebec during this period largely reflected the accent of Paris (whence most of the earliest French settlers came), certain regional groups also brought their particular dialects – Normand, Basque, Flemish, etc. Many of the unique accents and linguistic tendencies identified in Quebec today date straight back to this period, and the reign of Louis XIV.

As would be expected, however, these new settlers lacked words for many of the things they encountered. The fauna, flora, and native culture about them had no equivalents even in rural France, and so these early pioneers began to use the native terms for things particular to their new world. These settlers adopted Native American words for modes of transport and items (toboggans, moccasins, etc.) they had never before encountered. The same held true for names of new animals (wapiti, caribou, achigan, ouananiche), which were simply phonetic transcriptions of the Native American names. The name *ouaouaron* (giant frog) in fact, derives directly from the Native American onomatopoeia for the deep bellowing sound the creature makes. A good number of city names in Quebec were derived from the Native American names for places – towns such as Chicoutimi, Tadoussac, Natashquan, and others. Many other modern Québec terms also evolved from these early days, drawn from agriculture, fishing, and winter survival.

BRITISH CONTROL (1763–1840)

By the mid 18th century, the gradual arrival of British interests in the New World – most notably the 13 colonies bordering New France – began to significantly influence the original French settlers. The inevitable clashes between the two sides reflected the almost continuous state of war between their mother countries. The British and French approaches to colonization were notably different, however. Whereas the British remained in an essentially urban lifestyle, the French became familiar with the Native Americans, signed treaties with the tribes, and learned their languages. The significant linguistic overlaps with both English and the native tongues increased, and entirely new French words began to appear.

In September of 1759, the armies of British Major General James Wolfe and French General Louis Joseph de Montcalm clashed on the Plains of Abraham, just south of Quebec City. The British victory in this battle, and the fall of Quebec City to English forces, forever changed the future of New France. The other major French towns, such as Montreal, surrendered soon after. This victory prompted the departure of many of the wealthy French and French academics; those who did not return to France were on the whole tradesmen, craftsmen, and farmers, who had already put down familial roots in the New World.

Under the Treaty of Paris of 1763, the King of France surrendered the full rights to the territory of Canada to the British monarchy. This transfer of power opened the doors to a flood of new English-speaking European colonists, who brought with them new ideas, words, and dialects. Many new terms that developed during this period were based on the perception and integration of these new immigrants, including words such as *enfirouapé* (meaning "wrapped in fur"), a pejorative colloquialism for the wealthy English arriving in Quebec City in the post-war years.

Whereas Quebec's earliest commerce had been based on fur trading, the evolving social economy of Quebecers began to centre increasingly around agriculture. The years that followed the Treaty of Paris were marked by the establishment of the *seigneurial* system; some two hundred separate fiefs of land along the St. Lawrence River were owned by wealthy landowners, with the the land worked principally by farmers and tradesmen. These so-called *habitants* (those who lived and worked on the land) evolved the Québec tongue even further. The harsh winters, and the almost complete dependency on the St. Lawrence River, brought a spirit of strong independence – *un sens débrouillard* – to the culture and helped evolve a sense of *savoir-faire* that is noticeable in Quebec even today.

As the seigneural system continued to thrive, so did the deep roots of the Catholic theocracy that dominated much of Quebec, and its politics, for the century that followed. This religious influence markedly affected the language and brought many religious terms and words into common use.

THE BIRTH OF CANADA (1840–PRESENT)

As the Industrial Revolution sparked the rise of manufacturing, the process of Quebec urbanization accelerated, and the previously rural francophones began to increasingly answer the call of opportunity close to ports and commerce. By the late 19th century, Montreal had become Canada's premiere industrial centre, welcoming waves of European immigrants fleeing war in their homelands. Unfortunately, this quick urbanization caused tension between the British and French cultures. English – the traditional language of commerce – was being challenged for the first time as the province's language for business.

The middle of the twentieth century marked Quebec's transition away from the Catholic theocracy, which had effectively ruled its society for a century and a half, and toward a unified and integrated social structure. This "Quiet Revolution" – a sometimes-violent period denoted by a resurgence of pride in Quebec's French heritage – marked an increasing Francophone determination to publicly assert their identity, both in Canada and globally. A new sense of unity developed among francophones, culminating in the founding of the Parti Québécois and the referendums for Quebec independence in the years that followed.

The founding of the Office de la langue Française in 1961 – a governmental organization instituted to promote the use of the French language in the workplace and in general – for the first time formalized Quebec's intent to define the linguistic side of its French heritage. In 1969, then prime minister Pierre Elliot Trudeau's government introduced the *Official Languages Act*, defining both French and English as official languages of Canada and guaranteeing that all government services would be available in both tongues. Quebec, on its own initiative, declared itself a bilingual province and extended these rights at the provincial level as well. In 1977 the Quebec government enacted *Bill 101*, declaring French the official language of the province, making the province officially unilingual.

Today, the French and English languages coexist comfortably in most parts of Quebec. Although French is the official language of the province, many Quebecers are bilingual, communicating freely in both languages.

PRONUNCIATION

The common language spoken in Quebec – *Québécois* – is perhaps most typified by its distinct accent, which is about as different from Parisian French as North American English is from British English. There are about seven major discernable accents throughout the province, ranging from the deep Acadian of the north to the expansive accent of the Trois-Rivières region to the curt patois spoken near the American border. In general, the further out from the cities you go, the deeper and more historical the accent becomes. A good example of this is the pre-revolutionary "rolled" R sound, which is still heard in some of the more remote regions of Quebec.

Sensibly, much of the reason for this historical accent is that the language in Quebec did not follow the same evolutionary path as its mother language in France. Modern Québécois is hence a somewhat complicated mix of sixteenth-century accents combined with tendencies garnered from modern English. There are also many words and phrases that originate directly from accidental slurs of English words and phrases, such as *alldress* (all-dressed), *poutine* (put-in), and so on. The resulting language, while pleasing to the ear, can be very difficult to understand. To complicate matters further, Quebecers are renowned for their tendency to speak very quickly and often abbreviate or slur words together.

Below we provide an overview of the major differences in pronunciation and grammar between Québécois and International French.

General Pronunciation Tendencies

/a/ becomes /â/ or /ô/

The Québécois /a/ is often very deep and may more or less resemble an /o/ sound:

moi, là → mo<u>é</u>, l<u>ô</u>
là, je te dis → l<u>ô</u>, chte dzi
câlisse → c<u>ô</u>lisse

/i/ and /è/ become /é/ and /a/

Perhaps the best-known hallmark of the Québécois accent, this tendency directly reflects the standard pronunciation used in France prior to the French Revolution.

moi → mo<u>é</u>
toi → to<u>é</u>
merci → m<u>a</u>rci
merde → m<u>a</u>rde
chercher → ch<u>a</u>rcher
couverture → couv<u>a</u>rt

/e/ becomes /é/

dehors → d<u>é</u>hors
bedaine → b<u>é</u>daine
pesant → p<u>é</u>sant

/è/ becomes /é/ or /à/

mère → m<u>é</u>re
père → p<u>é</u>re
frère → fr<u>à</u>
j'avais → j'av<u>à</u>
poulet → poul<u>à</u>
vrai → vr<u>à</u>

/ê/ becomes /AY/

fête → f<u>AY</u>te
fève → f<u>AY</u>ve

/u/ becomes /eû/ in front of a consonant

bûche → b<u>eû</u>che
il fume → il f<u>eû</u>me

/i/ often becomes /é/ in front of a consonant

mille → m<u>é</u>lle
pipe → p<u>é</u>pe
risque → r<u>é</u>sque
vite → v<u>é</u>te

/ou/ becomes /ô/ in front of a consonant

courte → c<u>ô</u>rte
il pousse → il p<u>ô</u>sse
toute → t<u>ô</u>te

/in/ becomes a nasal /ain/ at the end of words

chemin → chem<u>ain</u>
jardin → jard<u>ain</u>

/i/ is softer

In general, the /i/ sound is pronounced more softly and quickly:

vite → vit
suite → swit

Slurs

/le/ and /la/ become /l'/

Québécois often drop the /e/ from *le* and the /a/ from *la* in front of words that start with a consonant, simply slurring the two consonants together:

> le camion → l'camion
> la chandelle → l'chandelle
> le tapis → l'tapis

/u/ becomes /i/ and /ou/ becomes /u/

Deeper vowels, such as /u/ and /ou/ are often replaced with sounds more comfortably produced in the front of the mouth:

> bas-culotte → bas-kilotte
> député → dépité
> soulier → sulier
> sous-sol → sus-sol

/j/ is pronounced as /ch/

The /j/ sound is often truncated and replaced entirely by a /sh/ or /ch/ sound:

> je suis → chwee
> justifier → chustifier

/re-/ becomes /ar-/

Québécois sometimes replace the /re-/ at the beginning of words with /ar-/:

> revenir → arvenir
> refaire → arfaire

And they often completely drop the vowels /i/, /u/, and /ou/, creating a liaison as necessary with the /z/ sound:

> arriver → arver
> camisole → cam<u>z</u>ole
> mes idées → me<u>z</u>dées

Affricates

Heard very frequently, affricates are the deliberate addition of an /s/ or /z/ sound after a /t/ or /d/ and a /il/, /y/, or /u/:

> Tu dis → t<u>s</u>u d<u>z</u>i
> dur → d<u>z</u>ur
> peinture → peint<u>s</u>ure
> tunnel → t<u>s</u>unnel

Diphthongs

Long and nasal vowels are often transformed into diphthongs, providing a more open and sometimes nasal sound than in International French:

> faire → <u>FAY</u>-yure
> banque → ba<u>w</u>nque

A particularly frequent case of this is the transformation of /or/ into /aor/:

> encore → enc<u>aor</u>

Clipped Endings

Québécois often completely drop the ends of words, especially those ending with /re/ and / le/:

genre → /gen/
article → /arteek/
par exemple → /par examp/

A final /r/ is also often transformed simply into an /é/:

tiroir → tiro<u>é</u>
mouchoir → moucho<u>é</u>

Verbs & Conjugating

The verbs *être* and *avoir* are pronounced quite differently by Québécois and are often almost inaudible in quick speech. Below is a table demonstrating English, International French, and common Québécois pronunciations:

Être (to be)

English	Int. French	Québec
I am	je suis	/shui/
you are	tu es	/tay/
he is	il est	/yay/
she is	elle est	/ellay/
it is	on est	/onay/
we are	nous sommes	(use "on" form instead)
you (*pl.*) are	vous êtes	/vzêt/
they are	ils sont	/iyson/
elles sont	/eson/	

Avoir (to have)

English	Int. French	Québec
I have	j'ai	/shé/
you have	tu as	/ta/
he has	il a	/ya/
she has	elle a	/ella/
it has	on a	/ona/
we have	nous avons	(use "on" form instead)
you (*pl.*) have	vous avez	/vzavé/
they have	ils ont	/ihyon/
	elles ont	/ezon/

Notable also is the Québécois tendency to use the simple future (*futur proche*) almost exclusively, instead of differentiating future events by using the verb *aller*. For example:

English	Int. French	Québec
I'll go a bit later.	Je vais aller tantôt.	J'irais tantôt.
You'll see him tomorrow.	Tu vas le voir demain.	Tu le verra demain.

Structural Differences

There are a vast number of differences between International French and common Québécois parlance at the structural level. Below is a summary of the elements most frequently heard in daily conversation that require explanation.

Double Words

Words can often be doubled for increased effect, especially in the negative:

> *Sa musique n'est pas fort-fort.* – His music isn't really that great.
> *Je l'aimais pas ben-ben.* – I wasn't really that fond of it.

English Usage

Québécois primarily use English to enhance an idea or to express an extreme. For example:

> *C'était vraiment bad.* – That was really the worst.

This also holds true for well-known English phrases that have not really been appropriated into common usage. If the French word seems overly complex, Québécois will often simply substitute the English word.

Les Autres

Québécois often replace *nous* with *nous autres* and *vous* with *vous autres*. This is similar in style to the English "you guys" or "y'all" rather than just "you." In the *nous* form, it's about the same as "we all."

Vous

One of the most confusing usage issues in Québécois is with whom to use the *vous* forms of verbs. Unlike their Gallic cousins, Quebecers are often significantly less formal, and so frequent use of *vous* is often more of a distancing measure than a politeness, especially among young people. As a general rule, introductions are made using the *vous* form and then people quickly switch to using *tu*.

Supressed Articles

The stand-alone particle *à* is often used to replace *ce* when referring to a time already familiar in context, such as *à soir* (this evening) or *à matin* (this morning).

When using *à* (meaning "to"), *dans*, or *jusqu'à*, the article that follows is often dropped, for example, *à gare* (*à la gare*), *à prochaine* (*à la prochaine*), *dans maison* (*dans la maison*).

Tenses

Québécois tend to use the conditional very frequently, especially when ordering or asking for something:

> *Je prend<u>rais</u> le bœuf* — I'll have the beef (when ordering at a restaurant)

Word-Level Changes

The /tsu/ construct

When asking a question, especially to an individual, Québécois tend to add an additional /tsu/, or replace "Est-ce que" with /s'tu/. For example:

> <u>*Tu*</u> *peux-tsu...* — Can you...
> <u>*S'tu*</u> *pour vrai?* — Is that for real?

Il and *Lui*

Québécois often drop articles and pronouns almost completely or relegate them to their final sound. For example:

English	Int. French	Québec
I've often said…	Je lui ai souvent dit…	<u>J'y</u> ai souvent dit…
There are three.	Il y en a trois.	<u>Y'en</u> a trois.

Là

Là is used in two different senses: to mean "there" (indicative) and also "now." Often heard is the expression *là, là,* meaning "as for that" or, literally, "there, now."

Ne... pas

In Québécois, either the *ne* or the *pas* can be omitted and still retain the negative sense of the sentence.

> *Je <u>ne peux</u> répondre au téléphone en ce moment.* — I can't come to the phone right now.
> *Je <u>peux pas</u> répondre au téléphone en ce moment.* — I can't come to the phone right now.

Québécois Prepositions

Sentences are often terminated with prepositions, similar to English:

> *Le gars <u>que</u> je sors <u>avec.</u>* — The guy (<u>that</u>) I'm going out <u>with</u>.

rather than:

> *Le gars <u>avec qui</u> je sors.* — The guy <u>with whom</u> I'm going out.

Sayings & Slurs

Québécois French contains a tremendous number of colloquial sayings that are often pronounced with such speed that it's difficult to understand the words and the root meaning. The lexicon below highlights some of the more popular Québécois sayings and slurs, which may frequently be heard in casual conversations.

Phonetic Pronunciation	Actual Spelling	Meaning
Aickssa?	Avec ça?	With that?
Anteka	En tout cas	Anyway
Anweille!	Envoye!	Move it!
Astheure	À cette heure	Now / Nowadays
Ben wéyon don!	Bien, voyons donc!	You're kidding!
Cammtoé	Calme-toi	Chill out / Relax
Check-moi le don!	Checke moi le donc	Look at that guy!
Chu danlune	Je suis dans la lune	I'm spacing out
Chudans l'marde	Je suis dans la marde	I'm in (deep) shit
Ch'tout fourré	Je suis tout fourré	I'm all mixed up
Chtsedsi (là)	Je te dis(, là)	I'm tellin' ya
Drette là	À droite là	Right there
Garsa!	Regarde ça!	Check that out!
Garledon!	Regarde-le donc!	Look at him!
Garladon!	Regarde-la donc!	Look at her!

Kesstufay	Qu'est-ce que tu fais	What's up? / What are you doing?
Métonque	Mettons que	Let's say that… / If it were that…
Mott'were t'aiyeur!	Je vais te voir toute à l'heure!	See ya later!
Pis?	Puis?	And so? / What's up?
Sad' lairasah	Ça a l'air à ça	It looks that way
S'tacause que	C'est à cause que	It's because
S'tassé	C'est assez	That'll do / That's enough
Tatu d'javu ça?	As-tu déjà vu ça?	Have you ever seen that before?
Tsu m'cré-tu?	Tu me crois-tu?	Can you believe it?
Vadon chier!★★	Va donc chier★★	You're shitting me!
Vadon toé!	Va donc, toi!	No way! / You're kidding!

Swears and Insults

S wears and insults (*jurons*) are used with such grace and flair in Quebec that they merit a separate chapter to correctly explain their usage and inflection. This chapter includes an overview of the most important words in this more "colourful" part of the Québécois tongue, their meanings, and an idea of usage. The reader is advised to use extreme caution with these words, since — as with oaths in English — they can easily offend people in the wrong context.

The Nouns

Most Québécois *jurons* are of religious origin, a historical ramification of the strong religious overtones that dominated the society through the eighteenth and nineteenth centuries. As such, most of the *jurons* come from objects from and around the ceremony of the Roman Catholic mass.

Baptême *n.f.* – Baptism
Câlisse *n.m.* – Chalice, the cup used for receiving wine in the Roman Catholic mass.
Calvaire *n.m.* – Calvary, the place where Christ was crucified.
Ciboire *n.m.* – Ciborium, a dish used for distributing the host in the Roman Catholic mass.
Crisse *n.m.* – Christ
Esprit *n.m.* – Holy Spirit
Ostie (hostie) *n.m.* – Host, the body of Christ in the Roman Catholic mass.
Sacrament *n.m.* – Sacrament

Saint Chrem *n.m.* – Chrism (holy oil)

Tabarnac (tabarnaque) *n.m.* – Tabernacle, the place where the host is kept.

Viarge (vièrge) *n.f.* – Virgin, a reference to the Virgin Mary.

Although each *juron* has a different meaning, they are more or less interchangeable from an expletive point of view. When used independently, they all roughly equal "shit!" or "goddam!" in terms of visceral effect.

Typical examples of uses include:

> *Crisse qu'y fait frette!* – Shit, it's cold!
> *Sacrament que ce gars-là est épais!* – Goddamit that guy is an idiot!
> *Câlisse que j'en ai marre!* – I've goddam well had it!
> *Ostie que je suis tanné!* – I'm so goddam sick of this!

To express frustration or swear lasciviously, Québécois often use combinations of *jurons*, since they're relatively easy to link together:

> *Ostie de crisse de tabarnac!*
> *Ostie de ciboire de calvaire!*

The word *ostie* is often added to sentences for emphasis, for example:

> *J'en ai marre, ostie!* — I've goddam well had it!

Additionally, almost any of the nouns can be used in combination with *être* to describe a state of being angry or upset:

> *être en tabarnac* — to be pissed off
> *être en câlisse* — " " " "
> *être en crisse* — " " " "

> *Là, je suis vraiment en tabarnac!* — I'm really pissed off right now!
> *La conversation qu'on a eue m'a mis en beau calvaire.* — The conversation we had left me furious.

The use of *jurons* with the partitive *en* generally means "a lot of":

> *J'en ai eu de la bouffe en tabarnac* – I had one hell of a lot of food.

There are, of course, almost infinite variations of each *juron*, mostly used to soften the sound. *Câlisse* and *tabarnac* are the ones most often changed to these less-offensive versions, roughly equalling "darn!" or "dammit!" in English:

> **Câlisse:** câline, calif, caltor
> **Tabarnac:** tabarnouche, tabarouette, tabarslak, taboire, barnak, tabarnane, tabarnic, taburn

Other frequently heard *petits jurons* — less offensive variants — include:

> Calvâsse
> Cibolle
> Maudit
> Maususse
> Mautadine
> Mautadit
> Jériboire
> Simonac
> Saint-Gériboire
> Saint-Sacrifice
> Torrieux

The Adjectives

Almost any *juron* can be used to augment the meaning of a noun or replace the word *très* (very). Note that the gender of the *juron* is always determined by the word it's modifying:

> *Ça, c'est une ostie de belle fille!* — That's one damn fine-looking girl.
> *Mon chum est un crisse d'idiot!* — My boyfriend is a goddam idiot!
> *T'es un criss de cave, toi* – You're a real idiot.

Oaths, especially *crisse* and *câlisse*, sound stronger when used to modify a noun, as in the above example, than when standing on their own.

The Verbs

Most *jurons* also have verb equivalents. For example:

> *Se crisser de (quelque chose) / Se câlisser de (quelque chose) / Se tabarnaquer de (quelque chose)* — To not give a damn about something.

> *Je m'en crisse s'il fait froid, je vais quand même aller skier.* — I don't give a damn if it's cold, I'm still going skiing.

To increase the effect of the words as verbs, speakers will add the word *contre* to the front of the verb: *s'en contrecâlisser, s'en contrecrisser*. For example:

> *Je m'en contrecâlisse s'il vient avec ou non.* — I really don't give a shit if he comes along or not.

Both *câlisser* and *crisser* can also indicate direction, in the sense of throwing or projecting something in a careless manner:

> *Je vais crisser ça dans les vidanges.* — I'm gonna throw it the hell out.
> *Je vais le câlisser dehors s'il continue de même.* — I'm gonna throw him the hell out of here if he keeps on like that.

Dictionary

For ease of reference, this dictionary section is structured alphabetically by general Québécois term, and these are then subdivided into the different ways each is commonly used.

English words are only included when there is a difference in nuance or usage from the standard English usage or when the frequency of their use makes their importance worth noting. Words that are essentially equivalent in both languages, such as car parts ("dash," etc.), or words adopted directly from English ("brunch" or "shack") are not included.

Words that are used in International French are noted with *Fr.* Such French vocabulary is generally included to help differentiate between the Québécois nuance and that of International French or to highlight words that are not commonly used in Quebec. However, bear in mind that in day-to-day language, words are often used with both the International French meaning and that particular to Québécois, depending on the context. For example, in International French *partir* simply means "to leave," but it can mean "to leave" or "to start" in Québécois.

Italicized phrases following an entry serve as usage examples. Those phrases offset with a dot (•) are idioms or phrases commonly heard in conversation.

Asterisks are used to denote strong or offensive terms. A single asterisk (★) indicates something that is a bit impolite, a double asterisk (★★) indicates something rude, and a triple asterisk (★★★) indicates something extremely rude or vulgar that should be avoided in polite company.

Due to the frequency of contractions of International French found in Québécois parlance (for example, *ben* rather than *bien*, *betôt* rather than *bientôt*, etc.), included herein are phonetic equivalents of commonly heard contractions and slurs to help make them simple to find and understand.

Abbreviations/Conventions Used

angl.	anglicism
cf.	see also
conj.	conjunction
contr.	contraction
def.	deformation
Engl.	English
ex.	example
expl.	expletive
expr.	idiomatic expression
f.	feminine
impl.	implies
incl.	including
interj.	interjection
Fr.	International French
lit.	literally
m.	masculine
n.	noun
orig.	origin
pl.	plural
pron	pronoun
sim.	similar to
v.	verb
v.i.	verb intransitive
v.t.	verb transitive

A

À *prep., Fr.* – to, at, about

* ❋ *à cause* – why
  À cause t'as fait ça? – Why did you do that?
* ❋ *à cause (que)* – because
  C'est pas d'à cause! – You're right!
* ❋ *à cette heure (là)* – now, at this point (*lit.* at this hour)
* ❋ *à cheval (sur les détails)* – hung up on the details (*lit.* on horseback for the details)
* ❋ *à date* – until now, up to this point
* ❋ *à la mitaine* – by hand (*lit.* by the mitten)
* ❋ *à l'année longue* – the whole year
* ❋ *à l'épouvante* – as fast as possible
* ❋ *à l'instant* – now, at (this) time
* ❋ *à mort* – to the extreme (*lit.* unto death)
  Il est pénible à mort. – He's unbelievably annoying.
* ❋ *à part (de) ça* – aside from that, additionally
* ❋ *à peine* – with difficulty
* ❋ *à pic* – irritable, ill-tempered
* ❋ *à soir* – tonight
* ❋ *À tantôt!* – See you later!
* ❋ *à terre* – exhausted, finished, dead (*lit.* on the ground)
  La batterie dans ma voiture est complètement à terre – My car battery is completely dead.
* ❋ *pas à peu près* – really, significantly
  Il est fâché, et pas à peu près! – He's really angry.

A-1 *adj.* – top notch, the best (pronounced as in English, /ey whun/)

(en) Abondance *n.m.* – a lot (of something)

Abreuvoir *n.m.* – water fountain, tap

Abrier *v.t.* – to cover, to shelter, to protect
As-tu abrié tes rosiers? Ça va geler ce soir. – Did you cover the rosebushes? It's going to freeze tonight.

Accommodations *n.f. pl.* – lodging, accommodations

Accommoder *v.i.* – 1. to receive, accommodate, host; 2. to help, to accommodate (someone)
L'hôtel peut accommoder presque mille personnes. – The hotel can accommodate almost a thousand people.

Accomplir *v.i., Fr.* – to accomplish
✹ *accomplir mer et monde* – to move heaven and earth, to overcome enormous difficulties (*lit.* to accomplish heaven and earth)

Accordant(e) *adj.* – accommodating

(s')Accorder *v.t.* – to get along
✹ *s'accorder comme chien et chat* – to fight non-stop (*lit.* to get along like cats and dogs)

Accotable *adj.* – easily competed with or defeated
Dans son métier, il n'est pas accotable. – He can't be beaten in his profession.

Accoté(e) *adj.* – hooked, attached
Je suis un homme accoté. – I'm an attached man.
✹ *être accoté* – to live together (out of wedlock)

Accoter *v.i.* – 1. to push or lay against; 2. to compete with, to challenge; 3. to attain the same level as (the competition)
Accote-toi sur moi, ça va brasser! – Hang on to me, this is gonna be rough!

Accoucher *v.i.* – to give birth
✹ *Accouche, qu'on baptise!* – Get on with it! (*lit.* Give birth so we can baptize! Often only the first word is used, and the rest understood, *Accouche!*)

Accoutumance *n.m.* – habit, custom

(d')Accoutumé *adv.* – typically, usually
D'accoutumé, il arrive vers cinq heures. – Typically, he arrives
around five o'clock.

Accrocher *v.t., Fr.* – to hang up; 2. to run into, to collide with
✹ *accrocher ses patins* – to end one's career, give up (*lit.* to hang
up one's skates)

Accroire *v.t., déf. "croire"* – believe

Accroire *n.m.* – belief
✹ *faire des accroires* – to make (someone) believe something
untrue, to deceive someone
*Elle m'avait fait des accroires qu'elle était experte, mais enfin du compte
elle n'en était pas du tout.* – She had made me believe that she was
an expert, but in the end she wasn't at all.

Achalage *n.m.* – annoyance, nonsense

Achalandé(e) *adj.* – congested, crowded
La rue était trop achalandée pour faire du vélo. – The road was too
congested to go bike riding.

Achalant(e) *n.m./f., adj.* – (one who is) annoying, bothersome,
exasperating

Achaler *v.t.* – to harass, to annoy, to disturb

Acharné(e) *adj.* – insisting, overly forceful; used when speaking of
people, not objects.

Achever *v.t.* – to make it to the end, to bring to a conclusion
Il faut qu'il continue à travailler s'il veut achever. – He needs to keep
working if he wants to make it.

Acrage *n.m.* – acreage, landsize

Actuellement *adv.* – currently, presently

La compagnie fait actuellement face à deux défis. – The company is currently facing two challenges.

Adon *n.m.* – luck, chance

On s'est croisés par adon. – We happened to bump into each other yesterday.

✸ *bien d'adon* – willing to get along, willing to help

Mon prof est bien d'adon quand je lui demande de m'aider avec tout ça. – My professor is really wiling to help when I ask him to give me a hand with that stuff.

Adonnant(e) *adj.* – likeable, friendly

(s')Adonner *v.i.* – 1. to be convenient, to be possible; 2. to get along (well)

On voulait assister à votre soirée, mais ça n'a pas adonné. – We wanted to join in your party, but it just wasn't possible.

Ta mère et moi, on s'adonne bien ensemble. – Your mom and I get along great.

✸ *ça s'est adonné que* – it turns out that

Adresse de retour *n.m.* – return address (for a letter)

Ad vitam aeternam *expr.* – without end (*lit.* to the eternal life; used to express frustration)

Son invité a parlé ad vitam aeternam; on était obligé de quitter avant la fin du souper. – His guest talked endlessly; we had to leave before the end of dinner.

Affaire *n.f.* – 1. thing, item; 2. stuff; 3. issue, problem; 4. business; 5. situation; not used as *Engl.* "affair," meaning extramarital relationship.

C'est pas de mon affaire, mais je pense que t'as tort. – It's none of my business, but I think you're wrong.

C'est une affaire un peu croche. – It's kind of a nasty deal.

Ramasse tes affaires, s'il te plaît, on s'en va. – Get your stuff together, please, we're leaving.

✱ *(une) drôle d'affaire* – strange situation

✱ *être en affaire* – to be in business, to be moving along

✱ *faire affaires* – to do business

✱ *faire l'affaire* – to be sufficient, to do the job

Tiens, du savon va faire l'affaire. – Here, some soap will do the job.

✱ *heures d'affaires* – business hours

✱ *paquet d'affaires* – bunch of stuff (to do)

✱ *(une) petite affaire* – a little bit, a hint

Affiler *v.t.* – to sharpen

Agace *see* Agace-pissette

Agace-pissette★ *n.f.* – tease (sexual sense)

Agasser *v.t.* – to bug, to irk, to bother

Âge d'or *n.m.* – elderly years (*lit.* the golden years)

Agneau *n.m., Fr.* – lamb

✱ *doux comme un agneau* – very polite, very gentle; usually said of someone very kind (*lit.* soft as a lamb)

Agrès *n.m.* – unattractive person

Aickssa *expr., déf.* *"avec ça"* – with that

Aiguiller *v.i.* – to direct, to point (in a direction)

Peux-tu m'aiguiller vers la pharmacie, s'il te plaît? – Could you point me to the pharmacy please?

Aiguiser *v.t.* – to sharpen

Aiguisoir *n.m.* – pencil sharpener

Aînés *n.m. pl.* – the elderly

Ainsi de suite *conj., Fr.* – and so on and so forth

Air *n.m., Fr.* – 1. air; 2. semblance, similarity

✱ *avoir l'air* – to seem, to appear

Ça a l'air qu'ils y vont quand même. – It seems like they're going anyway.

❂ *avoir l'air idiot* – to seem like an idiot

❂ *avoir l'air, mais pas la chanson* – to have it in principle but not in practice (*lit.* to have the tune but not the song)

❂ *avoir un air de bœuf* – to be in a bad mood

Aire de repos *n.m.* – rest area

Aisé(e) *adj.* – easy, in a relaxed sense

❂ *prendre (ça) aisé* – to take it easy

Ajouter *v., Fr.* – to add

❂ *ajouter de la job* – to add work (to something)

❂ *ajouter en plus* – to add (even more)

Ajustable *adj.* – adjustable

Ajuster *v.t.* – to adjust

Âldresse *see* Alldress

Alentour *n. masc.* – 1. surroundings, local area; 2. around

Est-ce qu'il y a un dépanneur dans les alentours? – Is there a convenience store around here?

Il y a plusieurs gamins alentour du char. – There're several kids around the car.

Alldress *adj., def. Engl.* "all-dressed" – with everything; used in the context of food (sandwich, pizza, etc.)

Je prends un hamburger alldress, s'il te plaît. – I'll take a hamburger with everything, please.

Allège *n.m.* – windowsill

Aller *v.i.* – 1. *Fr.* to go; 2. to go for, to accept

Je vais y aller pour le steak aussi. – I'll go for the steak too.

❂ *aller à l'épouvant* – to go at full speed

❂ *aller à malle* – to go get the mail

❉ *aller au batte* – to go to bat (for something or someone), to step up to the plate, to face an upleasant situation
❉ *aller aux toasts* – to score, to hit a goal
❉ *aller aux vues* – to go to the movies
❉ *aller virer à* – to head out to
❉ *au pire aller* – in the worst case

Allô *interj.* – hello; often used in the same sense as *bonjour* and not exclusively on the telephone, as in France.

Allophone *n.m./f.* – someone whose native tongue is neither French nor English

Allumé(e) *adj.* – 1. *Fr.* lighted; 2. a bit tipsy; 3. turned on, (sexually) excited

Allumer *v.* – 1. *Fr.* to light up, to illuminate; 2. to become clear or lucid; 3. to excite sexually, to turn on
   Arrête de m'allumer, toi! – Stop turning me on!
   J'ai allumé l'instant qu'il me l'a expliqué. – I understood the moment he explained it to me.

Allumette *n.f., Fr.* – match
   ❉ *gros comme une allumette* – as thin as a matchstick

Allure *n.f.* – set of desired qualities, allure
   ❉ *avoir (bien) de l'allure* – to be acceptable, good, valuable
   ❉ *ne pas avoir de l'allure* – 1. (of a person) to have bad judgement; 2. (of a situation) to make no sense
   Ça n'a pas d'allure, ta situation. – Your situation isn't pretty.

Amanchage *see* Amanchure

Amanché(e) *adj.* – 1. set, prepared; 2. stacked (for a girl), well-hung (for a guy)

Amancher *v.* – to be prepared, to be all set
   Cette affaire-là est super bien amanchée. – That business is really well-prepared.

✸ *(se) faire amancher* – to be had, to be taken advantage of

✸ *mal amanché* – badly off, unprepared

Amanchure *n.f.* – 1. trouble, mess; 2. badly done work

✸ *amanchure de broche à foin* – badly organized mess (*lit.* a haywire mess)

Amande *n.f.* – almond

✸ *gouter l'amande* – to be delicious (*lit.* to taste of almonds)

Ambitionnant(e) *adj.* – motivating, stimulating

Ambitionner *v.i.* – 1. to exaggerate; 2. to compete

✸ *ambitionner sur (quelquechose/quelqu'un)* – 1. to expect the unreasonable of (something/someone); 2. to take advantage of a situation

Moi, je trouve que t'ambitionnes bien trop sur ses capacités. – I think you're counting way too much on his abilities.

s'Ambitionner *v.i.* – to work hard, to outdo oneself

Ambitionneux(/euse) *n.m./f.* – ambitious person

Amen *interj.* – amen

✸ *jusqu'à amen* – without end, indefinitely

amérindien(ne) *adj.* – related to Native Americans

Amérindien(ne): *n.m./f.* – Native American person

Ami(e) *n.m/f., Fr.* – friend

✸ *ami de garçon* – male friend

✸ *amie de fille* – female friend

✸ *faire ami(e) (avec quelqu'un)* – to become friends (with someone).

(s')Amollir *v.i.* – to soften

Après ces années ensemble, il commence à s'amollir un peu. – After these years together, he's beginning to soften a bit.

Amour *n.m., Fr.* – love
> ❋ *tomber en amour* – to fall in love

An? *expr.* – huh?

Ancre *n.m.* – anchor
> ❋ *rester à l'ancre* – to await, remain motionless (*lit.* to remain at anchor)
> *Elle n'a pas bougé depuis le départ de son mari; elle reste à l'ancre.* – She hasn't moved at all since her husband left; she's in the same place.

Ange *n.m.* – angel
> ❋ *ange cornu* – one who misrepresents their good intentions (*lit.* horned angel)
> ❋ *beau comme un ange* – truly beautiful (*lit.* beautiful like an angel)

Anglais(e) d'Angleterre *n.m./f.* – British English (person or language); used to differentiate from a Canadian Anglophone

Anglo *n.m., contr.* – anglophone

Anglophone *n.m./f.* – native English speaker

Année *n.f., Fr.* – year
> ❋ *à l'année longue* – the whole year

Anniversaire *n.f.* – anniversary (marriage, etc.); note that in Quebec, the word *fête*, rather than *anniversaire*, is the word generally used for "birthday."

Annonce *n.f.* – commercial, public messages
> *Je vais y aller pendant les annonces.* – I'll go during the commercials.

Anteka *expr., def.* "en tout cas" – anyhow, in any case

Anweille (donc)! *expr., def.* "Envoye (donc)!" – C'mon! Move your butt!

Aouair *v.t., def.* "avoir" – to have
> *On va aouair un méchant fun à soir.* – We're gonna have a wicked-good time tonight.

Appel *n.m.* – call, phone call
   ❋ *appel à frais virés* – collect call
   ❋ *placer un appel* – to place a call

Applaudissement *n.m.* – clapping, cheers

Appliquer *v.i.* – to apply (for a job, etc.)

Apporter *v.t., Fr.* – to bring along
   ❋ *à apporter* – to go
   une pizza à apporter – a pizza to go

Apportez votre vin *expr.* – bring your (own) wine; a sign typically seen on Quebec restaurants whose liquor licence does not allow them to serve alcohol, only to have patrons bring their own.

(pas) Apprenable *adj.* – (not) able to be learned, (not) easily understood

Appui-livres *n.m. plur.* – bookends

Après *prep.* – 1. after, afterwards; 2. against
   Elle est fâchée après lui. – She's mad at him.
   Je vais la voir après. – I'm going to see her afterwards.
   ❋ *par après* – afterwards, next

Arachide *n.f.* – peanut
   ❋ *beurre d'arachide* – peanut butter

Aréoport *n.m., def. "aéroport"* – airport

Armoire *n.f.* – 1. cupboard; 2. closet

(en) Arracher *v.t.* – 1. to tear, to rip; 2. to have difficulty doing something; 3. to work hard
   Ma sœur en arrache avec son cours d'anglais. – My sister is really having problems in her English class.
   ❋ *arracher le cœur* – to be terribly upsetting *(lit. to tear the heart)*
   ❋ *être en arrache* – to be out of money; to be broke

s'Arracher *v.i.* – to defend oneself

Arranger *v.t.* – to set up, to arrange
Je t'ai arrangé un souper avec mon ami. – I set up a dinner for you
with my friend.
* *arranger le cadran (de quelqu'un)* – to beat (someone) up (*lit.* to
set [someone's] clock)

Arrêt *n.m.* – 1. stop; 2. stop sign; most stop signs in Quebec are
uniquely written with *ARRÊT,* rather than STOP.

Arrête donc! *expr.* – You're kidding!

Arriver *v.i., Fr.* – to arrive
* *arriver comme un chien dans un jeu de quilles* – to come crashing
into a situation (*lit.* to arrive like a dog into a bowling game)

Arsoudre *v.i., def. "résoudre"* – to arrive uninvited

Arsuer *v.i.* – to fog up (a mirror, window, etc.)

Articulé(e) *adj.* – articulate; used to describe a person

Arvenir *v.i., def. "revenir"* – to come back

Arvirer *v.i., def. "revirer"* – to turn around

Arvoler *v.i., def. revoler* – to fly apart

Assermentation *n.f.* – swearing-in (ceremony)

(s')Assir *v.i., def. "s'asseoir"* – to sit

Assurance-Santé *n.f.* – health insurance; typically used to denote
Quebec's health-insurance system

Astheure *expr., def. "à cette heure"* – now, nowadays

Astiner *see* Ostiner

Astineux(euse) *see* Ostineux(euse)

Ataca *n.m.* – cranberry (jelly)

Atchoum *n.m.* – sneeze

Atchoumer *v.i.* – to sneeze; from the onomatopoeia "atchoo!"

Atout *n.m.* – asset
- ✳ *avoir de l'atout* – to be skilled, to be handy (with something)

Atteignable *adj.* – attainable, able to be achieved

Attendre *v.i., Fr.* – to wait, to stay
- ✳ *attendre aprés (quelqu'un)* – to wait for (someone)
- ✳ *attendre du nouveau* – to be expecting a child; to be pregnant (*lit.* to wait for a new one)
- ✳ *attendre minute* – hold on a sec.

Attention à toi! *expr.* – take care of yourself!

Attoquer *v.i.* – to push against (something)

Attraper *v., Fr.* – to catch
- ✳ *attraper son air* – 1. to catch one's breath; 2. to be caught by surprise by something or someone

Attriquage *n.m.* – manner of dress

mal Attriqué *expr* – badly dressed

Au-delà (de) *prep., Fr.* – above, more than

Au juste *adv.* – anyway, actually
C'est quoi ça, au juste? – What is that, anyway?

Aubaine *n.f.* – sale, discount

Autant (que) *adv.* – as much (as)
- ✳ *en autant que* – insofar as

Autographier *v.t.* – to sign, autograph

Auto-patrouille *n.m.* – patrol car

Autoroute *n.f.* – highway; highways in Quebec are often referred to simply by their number (*ex.* "la 40" [Autoroute 40], "la 112" [autoroute 112], etc.)

Autre *adj., Fr.* – 1. other, further; 2. different, above; 3. more
  Il se prend pour quelqu'un d'autre. – He believes himself different.
  ✱ *ou autre* – or something else

Avancant(e) *adj.* – positive, favourable, forward-looking (*lit.* advancing)
  Un mec comme lui, pour une fille c'est pas avancant. – A guy like that doesn't do a girl good.

Avant-midi *n.m.* – morning (*lit.* before noon)

Avec – 1. *Fr.* with; 2. also
  Dérangez-vous pas, on va aller avec. – Don't worry, we'll go also.

Avoir *v., Fr.* – to have
  Il n'y a rien là. – Don't sweat it. It's nothing. It's not important.
  ✱ *avoir de la broue dans le toupet* – to have much work to do
  ✱ *avoir de la classe* – to have class, to be educated; generally used in the negative, to describe someone, as in *Pas de classe!*
  ✱ *avoir de la gueule* – to have character, to have a strong presence (*lit.* to have mouth)
  ✱ *avoir de la jarnigoine* – 1. to be a chatterbox, to be overly talkative; 2. to be intelligent
  ✱ *avoir de la mine dans le crayon* – to have a ravenous sexual appetite (*lit.* to have lead in the pencil)
  ✱ *avoir de la misère* – to have difficulty
  ✱ *avoir de l'atout* – to be skilled, to be handy (with something)
  ✱ *avoir de la visite* – to have guests (over)
  ✱ *avoir de l'eau dans la cave* – to wear pants that are too short (*lit* to have water in the basement)
  ✱ *avoir des bebites* – to have problems/issues (*lit.* to have bugs)
  ✱ *avoir des bidous* – to have money, to be rich
  ✱ *avoir des gosses*★ – to have balls, to be brave

✱ *avoir des idées croches* – to have bad (dishonest) thoughts

✱ *avoir des yeux dans la graisse de bines* – to be glassy-eyed (*lit.* to have one's eyes in the bean grease)

✱ *avoir des yeux pochés* – to have bags under one's eyes

✱ *avoir des yeux ronds comme des piastres* – to have eyes round like saucers

✱ *avoir des yeux (tout) croches* – to have squinty eyes

✱ *avoir des yeux tout le tour de la tête* – to have eyes in the back of one's head

✱ *avoir du bacon* – to have money, to be wealthy

✱ *avoir du chien* – to have determination or character (*lit.* to have some dog)

✱ *avoir du chiendent* – to have a lot of character

✱ *avoir du fun* – to have fun, to have a good time

✱ *avoir du guts* – to have guts

✱ *avoir du monde à la messe* – to be crowded (*lit.* to have people at the mass)

✱ *avoir juste le cul et les dents* – 1. to have no personality; 2. to be extremely thin (*lit.* to have just an ass and teeth)

✱ *avoir la bouche molle* – to slur one's words, most notably, after drinking (*lit.* to have a soft mouth)

✱ *avoir la chienne* – to be afraid, to be worried

✱ *avoir la débâcle* – to have the runs, to have diarrhea

✱ *avoir l'air* – to seem

✱ *avoir l'air de la chienne à Jacques* – to be badly dressed (*lit.* to seem like Jacques's dog)

✱ *avoir l'air simple* – to make a fool of oneself

✱ *avoir le cerveau en marmelade* – to be all mixed up (*lit.* to have jelly for brains)

✱ *avoir le cœur dans la gorge* – 1. to be nauseous; 2. to be on the verge of tears (*lit.* to have one's heart in one's throat)

✱ *avoir la couenne dure* – to be thick-skinned

✱ *avoir la coupe rude* – to be in a bad mood (*lit.* to have a rude cut)

✱ *avoir la face à terre* – to be annoyed, to be vexed

* *avoir le gros bout du bâton* – to have the advantage (*lit.* to hold the big end of the stick)
* *avoir la falle basse* – to have a long face, to be down
* *avoir la felle creuse* – to be very hungry
* *avoir la guedille au nez* – to have a runny nose
* *avoir la gueule fendue jusqu'aux oreilles* – to be grinning from ear to ear
* *avoir la langue à terre* – 1. to be exhausted; 2. to be very hungry (*lit.* to have one's tongue on the ground)
* *avoir la langue sale* – to have a dirty mouth (*lit.* to have a dirty tongue)
* *avoir la mèche courte* – to have a short fuse, to be quick-tempered
* *avoir la tête à Papineau* – to be very intelligent (*lit.* to have the head of Papineau)
* *avoir le feu au cul*★★ – to be furious (*lit.* to have fire in one's ass)
* *avoir le feu au passage* – to be furious (*lit.* to have fire in the passage)
* *avoir le goût (de faire quelque chose)* – to feel like (doing something)
* *avoir le moton* – to be choked up, to have a lump in one's throat
* *avoir le motton* – to have bucks, to have money
* *avoir le nez brun* – to be a brown-noser
* *avoir les baguettes en l'air* – to gesticulate wildly
* *avoir les bleus* – to be down in the dumps, to have the blues
* *avoir les deux pieds dans la même bottine* – to be clumsy, not resourceful (*lit.* to have both feet in the same shoe)
* *avoir les deux yeux dans le même trou* – to be exhausted; *impl.* to be staring at a point in space (*lit.* to have both eyes in the same hole)
* *avoir les mains pleines de pouces* – to be all thumbs
* *avoir les oreilles dans le crin* – 1. to be careful, fearing something or someone; 2. to be in a bad mood (*lit.* to have one's ears in horsehair)
* *avoir le sourire fendu jusqu'aux oreilles* – to be smiling from ear to ear

- *avoir les yeux dans le beurre* – to be tired
- *avoir le temps dans sa poche* – to take one's time, to go slowly (*lit.* to have time in one's pocket)
- *avoir le va-vite* – to have diarrhea; (*lit.* to have the go-quickly)
- *avoir mal à la cervelle* – to have a headache
- *avoir pour son dire que* – to think that (*lit.* to have for his say that)
- *avoir quelque chose pour une chanson* – to get something for a song
- *avoir sa botte* – to be involved in a sexual relationship
- *avoir sa journée dans le corps* – to have had a rough day (*lit.* to have one's day in one's body)
- *avoir son biscuit* – 1. to have one's proper compensation; 2. to have scored (in a sexual sense)
- *avoir son char* – to be fed up
- *avoir son voyage* – to have had enough, to be fed up (*lit.* to have one's trip)
- *avoir su* – had I known
- *avoir toute son idée* – to have a clear mind, usually said of a sharp-minded elderly person
- *avoir un coup dans le nez* – to have drunk a lot
- *avoir une crotte sur le cœur* – to have a chip on one's shoulder, to be prejudiced against someone
- *avoir une poignée dans le dos* – to be gullible (*lit.* to have a handle on one's back)
- *avoir un front de bœuf* – to be unflappable, to be unshakable (*lit.* to have the brow of an ox)
- *avoir un kick sur quelqu'un* – to have a crush on someone
- *avoir un air de bœuf* – to be in a bad mood
- *avoir une face de bœuf* – to be in a bad mood *(lit.* to have the face of an ox)
- *avoir vu neiger* – to have experience (*lit.* to have seen it snow)
- *avoir vu passer des gros chars* – to have experience (*lit.* to have seen big cars go by)
- *se faire avoir* – to be had, to be taken advantage of

Ayoye! *excl.* – 1. Ouch!; 2. Wow!

B

Babiche *n.f.* – animal skin
> ✱ *(se) serrer la babiche* – to tighten one's belt, to cut down

Babillard *n.m.* – billboard

Backer *v.* – to back up, support (financially or otherwise)
> *On a trouvé quelqu'un pour backer notre nouvelle business.* – We found someone to support us in our new business.

Backstore *n.m.* – storage, backroom

Baboune *n.f., Fr.* – lips
> ✱ *faire la baboune* – to pout

Bacon *n.m.* – 1. *Fr.* bacon, ham; 2. money, cash
> *Sors ton bacon, ca va coûter cher!* – Get out your money, this is going to cost quite a bit!
> ✱ *avoir du bacon* – to have money, to be wealthy
> ✱ *se pogner le bacon* – to goof off, to do nothing

Bad *adj., Eng.* – (extremely) bad; used to imply the worst possible case
> *C'est vraiment bad, son problème.* – His problem is really the worst.

Badloqué(e) *adj.* – unlucky

Bâdrant(e) *adj.* – annoying, irritating

Bâdrer *v.t.* – to bother, annoy
> *Ne me bâdre pas avec tes histoires.* – Don't bother me with your tales.

Badtripper *v.i.* – 1. to flip out, to be distracted; 2. to suffer; 3. to have a bad trip (drug-related)
> *Elle badtrippe depuis la mort de son père.* – She's been a mess since her dad died.

Bagosse *n.f.* – alcohol, particularly home-distilled alcohol

(se) Baigner *v.* – to bathe
- ✤ *baigner dans l'huile* – to go well, to go smoothly (*lit.* to bathe in oil)

  Quant au reste du projet, pour le moment ça baigne dans l'huile. – As for the rest of the project, for the moment it's going pretty smoothly.

Bain *n.m., Fr.* – bath, bathtub
- ✤ *bain tourbillon* – whirlpool, hot tub

Baise-la-piastre *n.m. /f.* – miser, greedy person (*lit.* coin-kisser)

Baiser *v.i., Fr.* – to kiss

Bajoues *n.f. pl.* – rosy cheeks

Balai *n.m.* – broom
- ✤ *aller au balai* – to leave someone alone
- ✤ *avoir le balai bas* – to be sad, dejected (*lit.* to have the broom low)
- ✤ *ballon-balai* – broom-ball, a popular Quebec game derived from hockey, played on foot using brooms and a ball rather than sticks and a puck.
- ✤ *fou comme un balai* – overjoyed, exuberant (*lit.* crazy as a broom)
- ✤ *jomper le balai* – to become pregnant (*lit.* to hop on the broom)

Balance *n.f.* – 1. *Fr.* scale; 2. balance (of money owed)

  Voici la moitié, je te paierai la balance demain. – Here's half, I'll give you the balance tomorrow.

Balancigner *v.i.* – to balance on a see-saw

  Les gamins veulent aller balancigner dans le parc. – The kids want to go see-saw in the park.

Balayeuse (électrique) *n.f.* – vacuum

  Veux-tu passer la balayeuse dans le salon, s'il te plaît? – Would you vacuum the living room, please?

Bal des finissants *n.m.* – prom

Ballant *n.f.* – balance, equilibrium

Balle *n.f.* – ball; often used to denote a responsibility, as in English. *Ouais, il m'a passé la balle là-dessus.* – Yeah, he passed me the ball on that.

Ballon *n.m.* – (inflatable) ball
- ✣ *crever le ballon de quelqu'un* – to burst someone's bubble
- ✣ *lancer un ballon* – to start a rumour, particularly a political one

Balloune *n.f.* – balloon
- ✣ *être en balloune* – to be pregnant
- ✣ *partir sur une balloune* – to go on a bender, to get drunk
- ✣ *péter la balloune* – to fail a breathalyzer (alcohol) test
- ✣ *péter la balloune de quelqu'un* – to burst someone's bubble
- ✣ *souffler dans la balloune* – to take a breathalyzer test (*lit.* to blow in the balloon)

Baloné *n.m.* – baloney

Balustre *n.m.* – balcony

Banc de neige *n.m.* – snowbank

Bandage★★ *n.m.* – erection

Baptême★★ *excl.* – shit (*lit.* baptism)

Barbier *n.m.* – barber (for men)

Barbot *n.m.* – drawings, markings, graffiti

Barda *n.m.* – noise
- ✣ *faire du barda* – to be noisy

Bardassement *n.m.* – annoying noise

Bardasser *v.i.* – 1. to be pushed, shoved, turned topsy-turvy; 2. to bang around (in anger)

Barfer *v.i.* – to barf, to throw up

Bargainer *v.t.* – to deal, to bargain
Il s'est bargainé un super de bon deal. – He bargained himself a great deal.

Baril *n.m., Fr.* – barrel
✱ *gros comme un baril* – obese

Barniques *n.f. pl.* – glasses, spectacles

Barré(e) *adj.* – barred, kept out
On risque d'être barrés d'ici si tu continues de même. – We are going to be thrown out of here permanently if you keep that up.

Barré(e) *adj.* – locked

Barrer *v.t.* – to lock
As-tu barré la porte? – Did you lock the door?

Barrure *n.f.* – lock, deadbolt

Bas(se) *adj., Fr.* – low
✱ *en bas de* – below

Bâs *n.m.* – socks, stockings
✱ *manger (ses) bâs* – to be uncomfortable with one's speech or action (*sim.* open mouth, extract foot; *lit.* to eat one's socks)

Bas-culottes *n.m. pl.* – panty-hose

Bassinette *n.f.* – crib

Bat *n.m.* – 1. bat. (baseball); 2. joint (marijuana)
✱ *aller au bat* – to go to bat for something or someone, i.e. to face an unpleasant situation

(se) Batâiller *v.i.* – to argue, to dispute

Bâtisse *n.f.* – building

Bâton n.m. – stick, club
> ✱ *tenir le gros bout du bâton* – to have the advantage (*lit.* to hold the big end of the stick)

Bavassage *n.m.* – gossip

Bavasser *v.i.* – to gossip, to talk behind someone's back

Bavasseux(euse) *n.m./f.* – gossipy person

Baveux(euse) *n.m./f., adj.* – arrogant, annoying, offensive (person)

Bazou *n.m.* – jalopy, heap
> ✱ *Aye, c'est un beau bazou, ça!* – Hey, nice car! (sarcastic)

Beau(Belle) *adj., Fr.* – beautiful, nice
C'est beau. – It's nice/good; often used in reply to an expression of thanks
> ✱ *beau comme un ange* – truly beautiful
> ✱ *beau smatte* – wise-ass, smarty-pants

Bébé la-la *n.m.* – one who acts like a child, crybaby

Bébelle *n.f.* – 1. toy. 2. thing, small object
Ramasse tes bébelles, on s'en va, là. – Pick up your toys, we're leaving now.

Bébitte *see* Bibite

Bec *n.m.* – small kiss, especially the double-cheek kiss popular in Quebec.
> ✱ *avoir le bec en cul de poule*★ – to have a continental French accent; typically refers to someone who retains a French accent despite several generations of family history in Quebec (*lit.* to have one's face in a hen's bottom)
> ✱ *bec sucré* – sweet tooth
> ✱ *faire le bec fin* – to be fussy about what one eats
> ✱ *se sucrer le bec* – to eat, particularly sweets

Bécosse *n.f., contr. Engl. back-house* – bathroom, toilet
* ❋ *aller aux bécosses* – to go to the bathroom

Bedaine *n.f.* – belly, gut
Aye, tu commences à avoir une vraie bedaine, là! – Hey, you're starting to get a real gut!
* ❋ *bedaine de bière* – beer belly
* ❋ *se promener en bedaine* – to go shirtless

Beigne *n.m.* – doughnut

Beignerie *n.f.* – doughnut shop

Ben *adj., adv., contr. "bien"* – well
* ❋ *ben-ben* – very
Ce n'était pas ben-ben bon, finalement. – It wasn't that great after all.
* ❋ *ben manque* – probably, perhaps
On va ben manque aller souper ensemble ce soir – We'll probably dine together tonight.

Bénéfic *adj.* – beneficial, advantageous

Bémol *n.m.* – negative thing, negative idea
Il y a juste un petit bémol : Jacques ne vient pas. – There's just one negative thing: Jacques won't be coming.

Bécher *v.t.* – to fall, to trip on something

Bequer *v.t.* – to kiss, to give a peck

Bétail *n.m.* – 1. beast (of burden); 2. difficult job or task
* ❋ *un ostie*★★ *de bétail* – a hell of a job

Bête *adj.* – rude, impolite
* ❋ *avoir l'air bête* – to seem unfriendly
* ❋ *faire un air bête* – to look (at someone) with contempt

Bête puante *n.m.* – skunk

Bêtise *n.f.* – 1. *Fr.* Nonsense, silliness; 2. insult, affront

Béton *n.m., Fr.* – concrete
- ✱ *couler (quelque chose) dans le béton* – to write (something) in stone, to fix something permanently (*lit.* to pour something in concrete)

Betôt *adv, contr. "bientôt"* – soon

Bette *n.f.* – 1. beet; 2. face
Lui as-tu vu la bette quand on l'a trouvé? – Did you see his face when we found him?

Beurrade *n.f.* – a buttery substance; used to describe anything that, similar to butter, can be smeared or slathered on something.

Beurre *n.m., Fr.* – butter
- ✱ *avoir les yeux dans le beurre* – to be tired
- ✱ *beurre de pinotte* – peanut butter
- ✱ *pédaler dans le beurre* – to make useless efforts (*lit.* to pedal in butter)
- ✱ *tourner dans le beurre* – to go nowhere (*lit.* to turn in butter)

Beurrer *v.t., Fr.* – to butter, to spread
- ✱ *beurrer épais* – to lay it on thick, to exaggerate
- ✱ *beurrer la face* – to show someone up, to rub something in someone else's face
Jean m'a beurré la face avec son nouveau travail. – Jean rubbed his new job in my face.

Beus *n.m. pl., contr. "bœufs"* – police, cops, pigs

Biberon *n.m., Fr.* – baby bottle
- ✱ *boire comme un biberon* – to drink like a fish (*lit.* to drink like a baby's bottle)

Bibite *n.f.* – 1. insect; 2. problem, issue
- ✱ *avoir des bibites* – to have problems/issues
- ✱ *bibite à patates* – 1. cockroach; 2. ladybug
- ✱ *bibite à poil* – small animal

Bicycle à gaz *n.m.* – motorcycle

Bidou *n.m.* – money
* ✻ *avoir des bidous* – to have money, to be well-off
Ça prend des bidous. – That costs real money.

Bien-être social *n.m., abbr. "BS"* – welfare

Bienvenue *n., adj.* – 1. welcome; 2. you're welcome
* ✻ *Tax de Bienvenue (n.m.)* – Welcome Tax; typically, taxes owed to the Quebec Government upon purchase of a new home.

Bière *n.f., Fr.* – beer
* ✻ *bière d'épinette* – spruce beer
* ✻ *bière en fût* – draft beer
* ✻ *bière tablette* – room–temperature beer
* ✻ *être de la petite bière* – to be without importance (*lit.* to be of small beer)

Bine *n.f.* – 1. bean; 2. face
* ✻ *avoir une drôle de bine* – to make a funny face, to make a strange expression
En goutant sa bière, il a fait une drôle de bine. – When he tasted his beer, he made a funny face.
* ✻ *être rond comme une bine* – to be completely sloshed, drunk (*lit.* to be as round as a bean)
* ✻ *être une bine* – to be nothing, to be small

Binerie *n.f.* – small, inexpensive restaurant

Bines *n.m. pl.* – (baked) beans
* ✻ *avoir des yeux dans la graisse de bine s*– to be glassy-eyed (*lit.* to have one's eyes in the bean grease)
À chaque fois qu'il la voit, il a les deux yeux dans la graisse de bines. – Every time he sees her, he gets completely distracted.

Binette: *n.f.* – face
* ✻ *avoir un drôle de binette* – to make a funny face, to make a strange expression

En goutant sa bière, il a fait une drôle de binette. – When he tasted his beer, he made a funny face.

Bisouner *v.i.* – to fiddle

Biscuit *n.m., Fr.* – cookie
* ❋ *avoir son biscuit* – 1. to have one's proper compensation; 2. to have scored (in a sexual sense)

Bitcher★★ *v.t.* – to complain, to bitch★★
Lui, il a bitché là-dessus pendant un bon 10 minutes. – He complained about it for a good 10 minutes.

Bizoune★★ *n.f.* – sexual organs, usually male but occasionally used for the female

Blanc *n.m.* – blank (space)
* ❋ *avoir un blanc de mémoire* – to draw a blank (speaking of one's memory)

Blanchon *n.m.* – baby seal

Blaster *v.* – to yell at (someone)
Je me suis fait blaster par ma blonde pour ne pas avoir apporté des fleurs. – I really caught it from my girlfriend for not bringing flowers.

Bleacher *v.t.* – to bleach, tint white
Demain, je vais me bleacher les cheveux. – Tomorrow I'm going to bleach my hair.

Blé d'Inde *n.m.* – corn on the cob (*lit.* wheat from India)

Bleu *n.m.* – 1. bruise; 2. state of being sad
J'ai toujours quelques bleus de ma randonnée à bicyclette. – I still have a few bruises from my bike trip.
* ❋ *avoir les bleus* – to be down in the dumps, to have the blues

Bleuet *n.m.* – 1. blueberry; 2. someone from the Saguenay/Lac-Saint-Jean region, which is well-known for its blueberries.

Blind pig *expr.* – speakeasy, illegal barroom

Bloc *n.m.* – 1. city block; 2. concrete or other support block
La gare est trois blocs par là. – The train station is three blocks that way.
Son char est sur les blocs depuis une semaine. – His car has been up on blocks for one week now.

Bloke★★ *n.m.* – English Canadian (pejorative)

Blonde *n.f.* – girlfriend

Blouse *n.f.* – woman's shirt, blouse

Bobépine *n.f.* – bobbypin

Bobettes *n.f.* – underwear, slip

Boboche *n.f.* – (badly made) object or item

Bœuf *n.m., Fr.* – 1. steer; 2. pig, cop, police officer
- ❋ *avoir un air de bœuf* – to be in a bad mood
- ❋ *avoir une face de bœuf* – to be in a bad mood

Boire *v., Fr.* – to drink
- ❋ *boire comme un biberon* – to drink like a fish (*lit.* to drink like a baby's bottle)
- ❋ *boire comme une éponge* – to drink like a sponge
- ❋ *boire comme un trou* – to drink like a fish (*lit.* to drink like a hole)
- ❋ *boire du fort* – to drink alcohol (*lit.* to drink some strong [stuff])

Bois *n.m.* – wood, woods
- ❋ *bois franc* – hardwood
- ❋ *bois mou* – soft wood
- ❋ *sortir du bois* – to make it out of the woods, to escape trouble
Il a presque fini, mais il n'est pas encore sorti du bois. – He's almost done, but he's not out of the woods yet.

Boisé *n.m.* – wooded area, glade

Boisson *n.f., Fr.* – drink

- *de la boisson* – alcoholic drink
- *être en boisson* – to be drunk

Boîte *n.f., Fr.* – box

- *boîte à lunch* – lunchbox
- *boîte à malle* – mailbox
- *boîte vocale* – voicemail

Bolle *n.f.* – intelligent person

Bombe *n.f.* – kettle

Bompers *n.m. pl.* – 1. bumpers (of a car, etc.); 2. boobs, breasts

Bon(ne) *adj.* – at least, a minimum (of something)
Ça va nous prendre une bonne trois heures de route. – It's going to take us a good three hours of driving to get there.

Bonhomme Sept Heures *n.m.* – the sandman

Bon Jack *n.m.* – a good fellow, a forthright person

Bonjour *interj.* – good day; used both as a greeting and a farewell
Bonjour, là – See you, now!

Bon vieux temps *expr., Fr.* – the good old days

Booker *v.t.* – to schedule, to book
Je vais booker une salle pour demain. – I'll book a room for tomorrow.

Booster *v.* – 1. to provide moral support; 2. to jump-start a car
J'ai besoin des câbles pour booster mon char. – I need cables so I can jump-start my car.

Bord *n.m.* – side
sur le bord de la maison – on the other side of the house

- *être sur l'autre bord* – to be pregnant
- *passer sur l'autre bord* – to die

Borné(e) *adj.* – pig-headed, stubborn

Borne-fontaine *n.f.* – fire hydrant

Bosse *n.f., Fr.* – bump
  * *rouler sa bosse* – to show one's wisdom (*lit.* to roll one's bump)

Bosser *v.t.* – to boss around, to play the head honcho; used differently from *Fr.* "*bosser,*" meaning "to work"
  Lui, il n'arrête pas de bosser tout le monde. – He keeps pushing everybody around.

Botchage *n.m.* – badly done work

Botcher *v.t.* – to mess up, to botch, to screw up

Botte *n.f.* – *Fr.* 1. boot; 2. screw (in a sexual sense)
  * *prendre une botte**** – to screw, to have sex with
  * *soule comme une botte* – completely wasted, inebriated (*lit.* as drunk as a boot)
  * *une bonne botte**** – a good screw, a good lay

se faire Botter *v.* – to be kicked
  * *se faire botter le cul** – to get kicked in the ass

Bottines *n.f. pl.* – shoes, footwear

Boucane *n.f.* – smoke

Boucaner *v.* – to smoke

Bouche *n.f., Fr.* – mouth
  * *avoir la bouche molle* – to slur one's words, most notably after drinking (*lit.* to have a soft mouth)

Boucher *v.t.* – 1. *Fr.* to stop up, to close; 2. to shut up
  Il s'est fait boucher pas longtemps après. – He was forced to shut up not long afterwards.

Bouette *n.f.* – mud, mire

Bougonneux(euse) *adj.* – grumpy

Bougrine *n.f.* – overcoat, outerwear

Bouilli *n.m.* – stew with meat and vegetables, similar to *Fr.* "*pot-au-feu*"

Boules★★ *n.f. pl.* – boobs, breasts

Bouleversant(e) *adj.* – staggering, bewildering, incredible
On a eu des nouvelles bouleversantes ce soir. – We had staggering news this evening.

Bouleverser *v.t.* – to shock, to bowl over, to blow away
Les nouvelles m'ont pas mal bouleversé. – The news shook me quite a bit.

Bourrasser *v.t.* – to be sharp, rude, bothersome

Bourratif(ive) *adj.* - filling (usually said of food)

Bourré(e) *adj.* – full (of food)

Bourse *n.f.* – purse, handbag

Boutte *n.m., def.* "*bout*" – 1. end, goal; 2. piece or part of something; 3. a while, a period of time
Je l'ai fait pour un boutte. – I did it for a while.
　❋ *au boutte* – 1. to the extreme; 2. to the end; 3. really good
Il l'a fait au boutte. – He did it right up to the end.
Il est au boutte, ton char! – Your car is the greatest!
　❋ *avoir/tenir le gros boutte du bâton* – to have the advantage (*lit.* to hold the big end of the stick)
　❋ *faire un boutte* – to leave, to depart, to blow out of (somewhere)
　❋ *sur le boutte de la langue* – on the tip of (one's) tongue

Boyau *n.m.* – hose
　❋ *boyau d'arrosage* – watering hose

Bozo-les-culottes *n.m.* – clown, idiot (*lit.* the clown with the pants)

Braillage *n.m.* – crying, weeping

Brailler *v.t.* – to cry

Braker *v.t.* – to brake, to slow down

Brancher *v.t.* – 1. *Fr.* to plug in; 2. to decide, to make up (one's) mind
Branchez-vous, les amis! – Make up your minds, guys!

Branler *v.t.* – to hesitate, take one's time
  * ✱ *branler dans le manche* – to hesitate when making a decision (*lit.* to hesitate in the handle)

Branleux(euse): *n.m./fem, adj.* – indecisive or hesitant (person)

Braoule *n.f.* – large serving spoon

Bras *n.m., Fr.* – arm
  * ✱ *coûter un bras* – to cost an arm (and a leg)
  * ✱ *huile à bras* – elbow grease, real effort
  * ✱ *sur le bras* – free, at no cost

Brassière *n.m.* – bra

Break *n.m.* – break
  * ✱ *prendre un break* – 1. to take a break; 2. to stop dating (romantic sense) someone temporarily

Bretelles *n.f. pl.* – suspenders, braces
  * ✱ *(se) péter les bretelles* – to boast, to brag (*lit.* to snap one's suspenders)

Bretter *v.t.* – 1. to dawdle, to waste time; 2. to drag on, to continue without end
Arrête de bretter et viens donc avec moi! – Stop wasting time and c'mon with me!

Breuvage *n.m.* – beverage, drink

Brisé(e) *adj.* – 1. *Fr.* broken, out of order, malfunctioning; 2. depressed, down (for a person)

Broche *n.f.* − 1. staple; 2. (wire) pin
- ✱ *amanchure de broche à foin* − badly organized mess (*lit.* a haywire mess)
- ✱ *broche à foin* − 1. haywire (thing or person), something out of order; 2. bailing wire (*lit.* hay staple)

Brocher *v.t., Fr.* − to staple, to attach

Brocheuse *n.f.* − stapler

Brosse *n.f., Fr.* − brush, hairbrush
- ✱ *prendre/virer une brosse* − to go on a bender, to get drunk

Broue *n.f.* − suds, foam
- ✱ *avoir de la broue dans le toupet* − to have much work to do
- ✱ *faire de la broue* − to blow hot air, to talk big

Brûlement *n.m.* − burning sensation

se Brûler *v.i.* − to burn one's self (out)
Je me suis vraiment brûlé pour livrer ça à temps − I really burned myself out to deliver that on time.

Brûlot *n.m.* − mosquito

Brun *n.m.* − a Canadian $100 bill

Brunante *n.f.* − sunset, sundown

Buanderie *n.f.* − laundromat

Bûche *n.f., Fr.* − log
- ✱ *se tirer une bûche* − to join in a conversation, etc. (*lit.* to pull up a log)

Bûcher *v.t.* − 1. to fell trees, to log; 2. to work hard

Bucker *v.t.* − to buck, to counter (something)

Bummer *v.* – 1. to beg, bum (money); 2. to hang around
Il avait du monde qui bummait du change dehors. – There were people bumming change outside.

Bumper *v.t.* – to move (something) out of the way, to bump
✱ *se faire bumper* – to be downgraded, to be pushed out

Butin *n.m.* – clothes

Buzzant(e) *adj.* – impressive, amazing

C

Ça *pron., Fr.* – this, that
- ✷ *ça doit* – that must be the case
- ✷ *Ça fait plaisir.* – It's my pleasure.
- ✷ *ça fait que* – so, therefore (*lit.* this makes it such that)
- ✷ *ça, là* – and as for that
- ✷ *ça paraît* – that's clear
- ✷ *ça prend* – that'll take; very similar to *Fr.* "il faut" and generally used to specify something necessary to identify a goal; also used in the reflexive (*ça me prends*)

  Ça prendra deux minutes de ton temps. – It'll take just two minutes of your time.

  Ça va te prendre une cuillère pour le manger. – You'll need a spoon to eat it.
- ✷ *Ça va (tu) bien?* – 1. How are you doing? 2. Are you OK?
- ✷ *C'est ça qui est ça.* – Things will be as they are.

Cabane *n.f., Fr.* – cabin, wood shack
- ✷ *cabane à sucre* – sugar shack, a cabin in the woods once used in the production of maple syrup and now mostly converted into restaurants serving traditional Québécois foodstuffs.

Cabaret *n.m.* – tray

  Le serveur a rangé les assiettes sur son cabaret. – The waiter placed the plates on his tray.

Cachette *n.f.* – hide-and-go-seek
- ✷ *jouer à la cachette* – to play hide-and-go-seek

Cadran *n.m.* – alarm clock

Cailler *v.i.* – to fall asleep

Caler *v.t.* – 1. to drink quickly, to swallow at a draught, chug; 2. to drown

  Vas-y, cale! – C'mon, drink up!

Câler *v.t.* – to order, to call
  On a déjà câlé trois pintes de bière. – We already ordered three pints of beer.
  * ✹ *câler l'orignal* – to puke, to throw up *lit.* (to call the moose)
  * ✹ *câler (son) bluff* – to call (someone's) bluff

Câline★ *expl., def. "câlisse"* – dammit

Câlique★ *expl., def. "câlisse"* – dammit

Câlisse★★ *expl.* – goddamn (*lit.* chalice from the Roman Catholic mass)

Câlissement★ *adv.* – goddam

Câlisser★★ *v.* – 1. to leave, to abandon; 2. to not care
  Je m'en câlisse. ★★ – I don't give a damn.
  * ✹ *câlisser (quelqu'un) dehors* – to throw (someone) out
  * ✹ *câlisser une volée* – to beat (someone) up

Calorifère *n.m., Fr.* – electric heater (radiator)

Caltor★ *expl., def. "câlisse"* – dammit

Calvaire★★ *expl.* – goddam (*lit.* calvary, where Christ was crucified)

Camion *n.m., Fr.* – truck
  * ✹ *camion de vidanges* – garbage truck

Camionneur *n.m., Fr.* – truck-driver, trucker

Camisole *n.f.* – woman's shirt, tank top

Camp *n.m.* – camp, camping place
  * ✹ *sacrer son camp* – to leave, to head out

Canal *n.m.* – channel, television station

Canceller *v.t.* – to cancel, nullify

Cancer *n.m.* – old car, rusted heap

Canisse *n.f.* – 1. milk drum; 2. can (of soda, beer, etc.)

Cannages *n.f. pl.* – canned products, conserves

Cannone *adj.* – striking, highly attractive (woman)

Canter *v.i.* – to fall asleep

Canular *n.m.* – candid camera

Capable (de) *adj.* – 1. *Fr.* able, capable of (something); 2. to stand, to put up with
> ✱ *Lui, là, je suis pas capable.* – I really can't stand that guy.

Cap de roue *n.m.* – hubcap

Capot *n.m.* – winter coat
> ✱ *capot de poil* – fur coat

Capotant *adj.* – unbelievable, phenomenal

Capoté(e) *adj.* – crazy, out of control

Capoter *v.t.* – to lose it, to go crazy, to get carried away
> *Oui, j'ai vu ce film-là. Ça m'a fait capoter!* – Yes, I saw that film. It made me completely lose it!
> ✱ *capoter (bien) raide* – to panic, to lose one's head

Carré *n.m.* – park, square
> ✱ *Carré Saint-Louis* – Saint Louis Square

Carreauté(e) *adj.* – checked, checkered
> *Il a mis un chandail carreauté.* – He put on a checkered shirt.

Carrément *adv., Fr.* – frankly, honestly (*lit.* squarely)
> *Je suis carrément crevé!* – Frankly, I'm bushed!

Carriole *n.f.* – carriage, cart
> ✱ *peau de carriole* – carriage blanket; typically refers to a blanket found in a horse-drawn carriage (*lit.* cart skin)

Carrosse *n.m.* – stroller, carriage

Cartable *n.m.* – binder, notebook

Carte *n.f., Fr.* – 1. card; 2. map
✤ *mettre (un endroit) sur la carte* – to put (someplace) on the map

Carter *v.i.* – to card (someone) to verify their age

Carte-soleil *n.f.* – Quebec health insurance card

Cas *n.m., Fr.* – case, situation
✤ *en tout cas* – in any case, anyhow

Cash *n.m.* – 1. cash (money); 2. cash register
S'il vous plaît, passez au cash après. – Please go to the checkout counter afterwards.
✤ *passer au cash* – to pay the price, to pay one's debt

Casque *n.m., Fr.* – helmet, hat
✤ *(en) avoir plein son casque* – to have enough (*lit.* to have one's hat full)
✤ *casque de poil* – fur hat
✤ *casque de bain* – shower cap

Cassé(e) *adj.* – 1. *Fr.* broken; 2. out of money, broke
✤ *cassé comme un clou* – completely broke (*lit.* broke as a nail)

Casse-croûte *n.m.* – small snack restaurant, often found on the roadside in rural Quebec

Casse-tête *n.m.* – puzzle (*lit.* head breaker)

Casser *v.i.*– 1. *Fr.* to break; 2. to break up, to split up
Ils ont cassé il y a trois semaines environ. – They broke up about three weeks ago.
✤ *casser la croûte* – to grab a bite (*lit.* to break the crust)

Casseux(euse) de party *n.m./f.* – bore, party-pooper

Catalogne *n.f.* – quilt

Catcher *v.t.* – to catch on, to get it, to understand
J'ai pas tout catché. – I didn't get it all.

Catin *n.f., Fr.* – 1. doll; 2. prostitute

Caucus *n.m.* – team discussion

Cause *n.f., Fr.* – reason, cause
✸ *à cause que* – because

Cave *adj.,n.m./f.* – moron, idiot (for an individual)

Cédule *n.f.* – schedule, timeline

Céduler *v.t.* – to schedule, to arrange a time for something

CEGEP *n.m.* – Quebec junior college

Cellulaire *n.m.* – cellular phone

Cenne *n.f.* – cent, penny
J'ai plus une cenne! – I don't have a cent left!

Centre d'achat *n.m.* – mall, shopping centre

Certain *adj.* – certainly, absolutely
Ça fonctionne, certain. – That definitely works.

Cervelle *n.f., Fr.* – brain, head, noggin
Je ne sais pas comment faire rentrer cette idée dans sa cervelle. – I don't know how to get that idea into his noggin.
✸ *avoir mal à la cervelle* – to have a headache

C'est en plein ça *expr.* – That's exactly it.

Chaise berçante *n.f.* – rocking chair

Chambalant(e) *adj.* – rickety, unstable

Chambre de bain *n.f.* – bathroom

Champ *n.m., Fr.* – field
* *être dans le champ* – to be in error, to be mistaken (*lit.* to be in the field)

Champlure *n.m.* – faucet, tap

Chance *n.f, Fr.* – luck
* *prendre une chance* – to take a chance

Chanceux(euse) *n.m./fem., adj., Fr.* – lucky, one who is lucky

Chandail *n.m.* – long–sleeved shirt, sweater

Change *n.m.* – coinage, loose change, spare change
* *prendre tout son petit change* – to make a tremendous effort (*lit.* to take all one's spare change)

Changer *v., Fr.* – to change
* *changer d'air* – to change one's mood or state of mind
Il doit changer d'air s'il veut s'amuser ce soir. – He needs to change his state of mind if he wants to have fun tonight.
* *changer d'idée* – 1. to change (one's) mind; 2. to take a break
* *changer quatre trente sous pour une piastre* – 1. to make no profit; 2. to change one thing for another of identical value (*lit.* to change thirty cents for a quarter)

Chansonnier(ère) *n.m./f.* – singer/song-writer

Chanter *v., Fr.* – to sing
* *chanter la pomme* – to flirt (*lit.* to sing the apple)

Chapeau *n.m., Fr.* – hat
* *parler à travers son chapeau* – to blow hot air, to speak without actual knowledge (*lit.* to speak across one's hat)

Char *n.m.* – automobile, truck
* *avoir son char* – to be fed up
* *avoir vu passer des gros chars* – to have experience (*lit.* to have seen big cars go by)

✖ *char de marde*✶✶ – deep shit (*lit.* a car of shit)
Je suis vraiment dans un char de marde avec ma blonde. – I'm in seriously deep shit with my girlfriend.

✖ *char de police* – police car

Charger *v.t.* – to charge, to bill
Combien charges-tu pour celui–là? – How much do you charge for this one?

Charge renversée *expr.* – collect (telephone call)

Châroéyer *v.t.* – (professional) transporter

Charrue *n.f.* – snowplow

Châssis *n.m.* – 1. window; 2. window pane

Chat *n.f., Fr.* cat
✖ *chat sauvage* – raccoon
✖ *Il n'y a pas un chat.* – There's no one (there).

Chaud(e) *adj.* – 1. *Fr.* hot, warm; 2. tipsy, slightly drunk.

Chaudasse *adj.* – tipsy, slightly drunk

Chaudière *n.f.* – 1. bucket, metal pail; 2. lunchbox

Chaudron *n.m* – cookpot

Chauffer *v.* – 1. *Fr.* to warm; 2. to drive
Tasse-toué, je veux chauffer un peu. – Move over, I want to drive for a bit.
✖ *chauffer les fesses* – to give a spanking (*lit.* to warm the buttocks)

Chauffrette *n.f.* – portable (electric) heater

Chaumière *n.f., Fr.* – cottage, country house

Chaussettes *n.f. pl.* – slippers

Chausson aux pommes *n.m., Fr.* – apple pastry
- ✱ *Et un chausson aux pommes avec ça?* – Would you like fries with that? (*lit.* Would you like an apple pie with that?)

Checker *v.t.* – 1. to verify; 2. to keep an eye on, to guard; 3. to check out, to look at

    Checke la fille là-bas! – Check out that girl over there!

    Je vais checker voir. – I'll check and see.

    Peux-tu checker mes bagages pour deux secondes? – Can you keep an eye on my bags for a few seconds?

Chemin *n.m., Fr.* – path, road, way
- ✱ *chemin de garnotte* – gravel road
- ✱ *chemin de gravelle* – gravel road

Chèque de voyage *n.f* – traveller's cheque

Chevreuil *n.m.* – deer, buck

Chez *prep.* – at
- ✱ chez-nous – my house; Québécois almost always use the plural form (chez-nous, chez-vous, chez-eux), even when speaking about a residence with only one person.

    J'm'en va chez nous. – I'm going back to my place.

Chiâleux(euse) *adj. & n.m./fem.* – grumpy, crabby, ill-tempered

Chiâler *v.i.* – to complain, to bitch; in France, this word implies crying or weeping, not complaining.

Chiard *n.m.* – 1. beef stew; 2. difficulty, a complex issue
- ✱ *être dans un beau chiard* – to be in trouble (*lit.* to be in a nice stew)

Chicane *n.f.* – argument, dispute
- ✱ *chicane de ménage* – household argument
- ✱ *pogner une chicane* – to have an argument

Chicoter *v.i.* – to bother, to disturb

    Ça m'a chicoté toute la nuit. – It bothered me all night long.

Chien(ne) *adj.* – 1. mean; 2. chicken, fraidy-cat
Il pourrait, mais il est trop chien pour le faire. – He could, but he's too afraid to do it.
- ✳ *avoir du chien* – to have determination or character (*lit.* to have some dog)
- ✳ *son chien est mort* – to be done-in, to be finished (*lit.* his dog is dead)

Chiendent *n.m.* – weeds, dog's-tooth grass
- ✳ *avoir du chiendent* – to have a lot of character

Chienne★★ *n.f., Fr.* – bitch; used for both a female dog and, as in English, a derogatory term for a girl.
- ✳ *avoir la chienne* – to be afraid, to be worried
- ✳ *avoir l'air de la chienne à Jacques* – to be badly dressed; *lit.* to look like Jacques's dog

Chier★★★ *v.* – *Fr.* to shit
- ✳ *chier de l'or en barre*★ – to believe oneself to be special (*lit.* to shit bars of gold)
- ✳ *chier dans (ses) culottes*★★ – to be afraid, to shit in (one's) pants
- ✳ *faire chier* – to suck, to be bad
Ça fait chier! – That sucks!
- ✳ *Va chier!* – Piss off!
- ✳ *Va chier un lunch au large!*★★ – Go take a fuckin' hike!

Chieux(euse) *adj., n.m./fem.* – scared, coward

Chigner *v.i.* – to whine, to snivel

Chiottes★★ *n.f. pl.* – toilet, bathroom (*lit.* the shitters)

Chnolles★★ *n.f. pl.* – balls, testicles

Chnoute★★ *n.f.* – shit
Cette affaire-là, c'est juste de la chnoute. – That thing is a total piece of shit.

Choqué(e) *adj.* – angry, perturbed

(se) Choquer *v.i.* – to become angry

Chose bine *pron.* – what's-his-name
    Je parlais avec chose bine, là. – I was talking with what's-his-name.

Chotte *n.f.* – shot
    ✱ *boire d'une chotte* – to gulp down
    ✱ *faire (quelque chose) d'une (seule) chotte* – to do (something) all at once, do (something) in a single shot

Chou *n.m.* – 1. cabbage; 2. darling (term of endearment)

Chouclaques *n.m.* – sneakers, running shoes

Chromo★★ *n.m.* – troll, ugly person

Chu *pron., contr. "je suis"* – I am

Chum *n.m.* – 1. boyfriend (female referring to male); 2. friend (male referring to male)
    ✱ *être ben chum avec (quelqu'un)* – to be really chummy with (someone)

Ciarge *n.f.* – slang, patois

Ciboire *expl.* – Goddamit

Cigne *n.m.* – kitchen sink

Cimonaque *expl.* – dammit

Cinquante-sous *n.m* – fifty-cent piece

Circulaire *n.f.* – advertisement, junk mail
    Je reçois constamment des circulaires sous ma porte. – I'm constantly getting advertisements under my door.

Citron *adj., n.m., Fr.* – lemon; often used as a pejorative word for a car.
    ✱ *se faire passer un citron* – to be handed a lemon

Clair(e) *adj.* – clear, lucid

Clairer *v.t.* – to clear up, finish, clear out
On va clairer de l'espace pour les nouveaux meubles. – We'll make some space for the new furniture.

✷ *se faire clairer* – to be thrown out (of a bar, etc.)

Clancher *v.i.* – 1. to accelerate violently; 2. to work well; 3. to take off
Oui, notre business commence à clancher. – Yes, our business is really starting to take off.

Claque *n.f., Fr.* – slap

✷ *donner la claque* – to give it your best

Claques *n.f. pl.* – rubbers, boots

Clavarder *v.i., contr. "clavier" and "bavarder"* – to chat on the Internet

Clenche *n.f.* – latch (of a door, etc.)

Cliquer *v.i.* – 1. to make sense, to click (an idea); 2. to work well
Ça clique! – That works!
Ça clique! – That works!
Je lui ai expliqué cinq fois, mais il n'a pas encore cliqué. – I've explained it to him five times, but it still hasn't clicked.

Clôture *n.f., Fr.* – gate

✷ *sauter la clôture* – to cheat on one's spouse (*lit.* to jump the gate)

Clou *n.m., Fr.* – nail

✷ *cassé comme un clou* – broke, penniless (*lit.* broke as a nail)

✷ *cogner des clous* – to be nodding off (to sleep) (*lit.* to drive nails in)

✷ *tomber comme des clous* – to rain heavily (*lit.* to fall like nails)

Coche *n.f.* – groove, cut, notch

✷ *monter d'une coche* – to go up a notch

Cochon *n.m., Fr.* – pig

✷ *prendre la passe du cochon qui tousse* – to cut corners, to take a shortcut (*lit.* to take the way of the coughing pig)

Cochon(ne) *adj.* – dirty (in a sexual sense) (*lit.* pig-like)

Cocotte *n.f.* – pine cone

Code régional *n.m.* – area code (telephone)

Cœur *n.m., Fr.* – heart
> ✻ *avoir une crotte sur le cœur* – to have a chip on one's shoulder, to be prejudiced against someone

Coin *n.m., Fr.* – corner
> ✻ *tourner les coins ronds* – to steer clear of problems (*lit.* to turn rounded corners)

Coincé(e) *adj., n.m./fem.* – 1. narrow-minded (person); 2. stuck, backed into a corner (literally or figuratively)
> *Ce gars-là, je l'ai toujours trouvé un peu coincé.* – I've always found that guy to be kind of narrow-minded.

Col-bleu *n.m.* – blue-collar (worker)

Collant(e) *adj.* – clingy, hanger-on (for a person)

Colle *n.f., Fr.* – glue
> ✻ *ne pas valoir de la colle* – to be worthless, to be of bad quality (*lit.* to not be worth glue)

(se) Coller *v.* – 1. *Fr.* to stick, to glue; 2. to curl up with, to snuggle against
> ✻ *coller comme la misère sur le pauvre monde* – to be firmly attached to something (*lit.* to stick as misery to the poor)

Colleux(euse) *n.m./f/* – 1. hug; 2. clingy person

Coloc *n.m./fem., contr.* "*colocataire*" – roommate, joint tenant

Colon *n.m., adj.* – 1. idiot, moron; 2. bumpkin, redneck; 3. tasteless, gaudy

Combines *n.f. pl.* – long-johns, full-length underwear

Combler *vt* – to fill, to provide

Commande *n.f.* – order
   ✸ *faire la commande* – to go (food) shopping

Comme *conj., Fr.* – as
   ✸ *comme du monde* – as everyone else (is) (*lit.* as other folks)
   ✸ *comme quoi que* – given that

Comment *adv.* – 1. *Fr.* how; 2. how much
   Comment ça va faire? – How much will that be?

Compagnie *n.f.* – company

Compléter *v.t., Fr.* – to fill out, complete
   S'il vous plaît, compléter le formulaire. – Please fill out the form.

Compote *n.m., Fr.* – 1. compost (bin); 2. fruit jam
   ✸ *tomber en compote* – to fall to pieces (*lit.* fall into fruit jam)

Comprenable *adj.* – comprehensible, understandable

Comptable agréé(e) *n.m./f.* – chartered accountant

Comptant *n.m., Fr.* – cash
   ✸ *payer comptant* – to pay in cash

Comptoir *n.m.* – counter
   Je l'ai mis sur le comptoir. – I put it on the counter.

Comté *n.m.* – county

Concerné(e) *adj.* – involved, concerned

Concerner *v.i.* – to be involved, to be concerned with (something)
   ✸ *en autant que ça me concerne* – insofar as it involves me
   ✸ *en autant que je sois concerné* – as far as I'm concerned

Confortable *adj.* – comfortable, at ease

Congédier *v.t.* – to fire, to let go of an employee (*lit.* to vacation)

Conjoint(e) *n.m./f.* – life partner

Connecter *v.t.* – to connect, plug together

Conservateur(trice) *n.m./fem., adj.* – moderate, conservative

(se) Contrecâlisser** *v.i.* – to not give a shit, to not care, to ignore
Je m'en contrecâlisse s'il vient ou pas. – I don't give a shit if he comes along or not.

(se) Contrecrisser** *v.i.* – to not give a shit, to not care, to ignore
Je m'en contrecrisse s'il vient ou pas. – I don't give a shit if he comes along or not.

Contrôle *n.m., Fr.* – control.
✱ *sous contrôle* – under control

Contrôler *v.t.* – to control; different from International French, in which it means to verify or insure

Coquel'œil *adj.* – blind as a bat

Coquerelle *n.f.* – cockroach

Coqueron *n.m.* – tiny apartment, a closet

Corde à linge *n.f.* – washline, clothesline
✱ *passer la nuit sur la corde à linge* – to sleep badly (*lit.* to sleep on the clothesline)

Corps *n.m., Fr.* – body
✱ *veillée au corps* – a funeral wake (ceremony)

Correct(e) *adj.* – okay, successful, in order, correct, acceptable
✱ *C'est-tu correct?* – Is it ok?

Correspondre *v.i.* – to contact, to correspond (with someone)

Cossin *n.m.* – small thing, object

Costaud(e) *adj.* – stocky, well-built, strong (for a person)
Peut-être qu'il est petit, mais il est costaud! – He might be small, but he's built!

Costume de bain *n.m.* – bathing suit

Cotation *n.f.* – quotation, statement of price

Côté *n.m.* – side
❋ *être sur l'autre coté* – to be pregnant
❋ *passer sur l'autre coté* – to die

Côtes levées *n.f. pl.* – spareribs

Coton *n.m., Fr.* – cotton
❋ *être au coton* – 1. to be at the end of one's means or patience; 2. to be exhausted
❋ *faire coton* – to be pathetic

(se) Coucher *v.t., Fr.* – to go to bed
❋ *se coucher les fesses à l'air* – to sleep butt-naked (*lit.* to sleep with one's cheeks to the wind)

Coude *n.m., Fr.* – elbow
❋ *Se lever le coude* – to have several beers (*lit.* to lift one's elbow)

Coudon *expr., def.* "écoute donc" – c'mon

Couenne *n.f.* – skin
❋ *avoir la couenne dure* – to be thick–skinned

Coulante *adj.* – slippery (surface, etc.)

Couler *v.i.* – 1. *Fr.* to run, to drip (for a liquid); 2. to blow it, to fail
Je crois qu'il va encore couler son affaire. – I think he's going to blow it again.
❋ *couler (quelque chose) dans le béton* – to cast (something) in stone

Coulisse *n.f.* – drippings

Coup *n.m.* – 1. a drink; 2. *Fr.* a blow
Il a reçu deux coups à la tête. – He took two blows to the head.
❋ *avoir un coup dans le nez* – to have drunk a lot
❋ *boire un coup* – to grab a drink

❋ *coup de fil* – phone call

❋ *lâcher un coup de fil* – to give someone a phone call

Couper *v.t., Fr.* – to cut, to reduce

❋ *couper le prix* – to cut the price

Courâiller *v.i.* – 1. to chase skirts, to womanize; 2. to run errands

Courâilleux *n.m.* – skirt-chaser, womanizer

Cour à scrap *n.m.* – junkyard

Coureux(euse) *n.m./f., adj* – one who likes to travel

❋ *gang de coureux* – group that enjoyes travel together

Courir *v.i., Fr.* – to run

❋ *courir la galipote* – to galivant, to chase women

Courriel *n.m.* – electronic mail (email)

Coutellerie *n.f.* – cutlery, utentils

Coûter *v.i., Fr.* – to cost

❋ *couter la peau des fesses* – to cost a fortune (*lit.* to cost the skin off your butt)

❋ *coûter les yeux de la tête* – to cost a fortune (*lit.* to cost the eyes from your head)

❋ *coûter un bras* – to cost an arm (and a leg)

Couvert *n.m.* – cover, lid

Couverte *n.f.* – blanket, cover

Crampant(e) *adj.* – funny, hilarious (*lit.* causing cramps)

Crampé(e) *adj.* – highly amused (*lit.* to have a cramp)
J'étais crampé à cause de ce qu'il a dit. – I was doubled over by what he said.

Cramper *v.i.* – to laugh to the point of doubling over, to laugh to the point of tears

Crapaud(e) *adj.* – wily, crafty, untrustworthy
En affaires, il est crapaud. – In terms of business, he's not very trustworthy.

Crayon *n.m.* – pen, pencil
   ✷ *avoir de la mine dans le crayon*✶ – to have a ravenous sexual appetite (*lit.* to have lead in the pencil)

Cré(e) *adj.* – good old; used to refer affectionately or ironically to a person and/or their traits.
   Cré Jean, il est venu nous aider ènéouai! – Good ol' Jean, he came to help us anyway!

Crèche *n.f.* – orphanage; whereas *crèche* means "daycare" in France, Québécois generally use *garderie* instead.

Crémage *n.m.* – icing

Crème à barbe *n.f.* – shaving cream

Crème glacée *n.f.* – ice cream

Crémone *n.f.* – long, knit scarf

Crère *v., déf. "croire"* – believe
   Crée-moi, je suis sincère – Believe me, I'm not kidding.
   Tu dois me crère! – You gotta believe me!

Cretons *n.m. pl.* – pâté made from veal or pork, usually eaten at breakfast

Creux(euse) *adj.* – 1. *Fr.* deep; 2. far away, isolated

Crevant(e) *adj* – hilarious, really funny
   C'est un gars crevant. – He's a really funny guy.

Crever *v.i., Fr.* – 1. to burst or deflate; 2. to die, to fail
   ✷ *crever le ballon de quelqu'un* – to burst someone's bubble

Criard *n.m.* – car horn

Crime! *expr.* – Heck!

Crin *n.m., Fr.* – horsehair
* ❋ *avoir les oreilles dans le crin* – 1. to be careful, fearing something or someone; 2. to be in a bad mood (*lit.* to have one's ears in horsehair)

Crinqué(e) *adj., n.m. /f.* – pissed off, angry (person)

Crinquer *v.t.* – to crank, to wind up; used both in the figurative ("to crank someone up") and literal ("to crank a winch") senses.
Il l'a rendu complètement crinqué sur l'idée de prendre sa poste lors de son départ. – He got her totally wound up about taking over his position when he leaves.

Crise *n.f., Fr.* – 1. crisis; 2. fit
* ❋ *piquer une crise* – to throw a fit; different from International French, in which this means "to faint."

Crissant(e)★ *adj.* – a pain in the ass

Crisse★★ *expl.* – Goddamit (*lit.* Christ)
* ❋ *Ben, crisse!* – Oh, hell!
* ❋ *Petit crisse* – traitor, two-faced person

Crissement★ *adv.* – (one hell of) a lot

Crisser★ *v.i.* – 1. to leave
* ❋ *crisser dehors* – to throw (someone/something) out
* ❋ *crisser son camp* – to leave, to blow out of somewhere
* ❋ *crisser une volée* – to teach someone a lesson (with physical force)
S'il n'arrête pas de me faire chier, je vais lui crisser une volée bientôt!★ – If he doesn't stop pissing me off, I'm going to teach his ass a lesson pretty soon!
* ❋ *Je m'en crisse!* – I don't give a damn!
Crisse-moi la patience! – Beat it! Leave me the heck alone!
* ❋ *se crisser de (quelque chose)* – to not give a damn about (something)

Croche *adj., Fr.* – bad, nasty, dishonest

- *avoir des idées croches* – to have bad/dishonest thoughts
- *avoir les yeux (tout) croches* – to have squinty eyes
- *être tout croche* – 1. to be bad; 2. to be dirty, distasteful; 3. to be hung over
- *penser croche* – to think dirty (in a sexual sense)
- *se sentir (tout) croche* – to feel (really) bad, to be unhappy

(se) Crosser★★★ *v.i.* – 1. to wank, to masturbate; 2. to counter, to go against

- *se faire crosser* – to be screwed over, to be betrayed

Je ne veux pas me faire crosser là-dessus. – I don't want to be screwed over on this.

Crosseur(euse)★ *n.m./fem.* – cheat, traitor, hypocrite

Cru(e) *adj., Fr.* – raw; often used to describe the weather (raw and cold).

Cruiser *v.t.* – 1. to hit on someone, to make a pass at someone; 2. to go out cruising

Il n'a pas arrêté de la cruiser toute la soirée. – He didn't stop hitting on her all night.

Cruising-bar *expr.* – meat-market, pick-up joint

Cul *n.m., Fr.* – 1. end; 2. ass★★

- *avoir juste le cul et les dents* – 1. to have no personality; 2. to be extremely thin (*lit.* to have just ass and teeth)
- *avoir le bec en cul de poule★* – to have a continental French accent; typically refers to someone who retains a French accent despite several generations of family history in Quebec (*lit.* to have one's face in a hen's bottom)
- *avoir le trou de cul en dessous du bras★★* – to be exhausted (*lit.* to have one's asshole under the arm)
- *se faire botter le cul★* – to get kicked in the ass

Culottes *n.f.* – pants

- *les culottes à terre* – with (one's) pants down

D

D'abord *adv.* – 1. *Fr.* first; 2. already
Dis-moi, d'abord! – Tell me, already!
Je vais tinker mon char d'abord. – I'm going to fill up my car first.
OK d'abord! – OK then, that's fine!
✲ *d'abord que* – since, given that
D'abord que tu y vas, moi j'ai pas besoin. – Since you're going, I don't need to.

Dactylo *n.m.* – typewriter

Danse *n.f., Fr.* – dance
✲ *danse carrée* – square dance

Dash *n.m.* – dashboard (of a car)
✲ *fesser dans le dash* – to be surprising, to be unexpected

Date *n.m.* – 1. *Fr.* date (day); 2. date, romantic meeting
✲ *à date* – until now, up to this point

Débâcle *n.m., Fr.* – debacle, messy situation
✲ *avoir le débâcle* – to have the runs, to have diarrhea

Débalancé(e) *adj.* – out of whack, unbalanced

Débalancer *v.t.* – to throw out of whack, to unbalance

Débarbouillette *n.f.* – washcloth

Débarque *n.f.* – fall
✲ *prendre une débarque* – to fall down/off

Débarquer *v.* – 1. to take down; 2. to exit from a vehicle; 3. to quit
On est débarqués de son char juste à côté de la piste. – We got out of the car right next to the ski slope.
Tout de même, Jacques va débarquer du conseil d'administration l'année prochaine. – Even so, Jacques will leave the board of directors next year.

Débarrer *v.t.* – to unlock
Je viens de débarrer la porte. – I just unlocked the door.

Débâtir *v.t.* – to demolish, to knock down (*lit.* to unbuild)
Ils vont débâtir la vieille église demain. – They're going to demolish the old church tomorrow.

(se) Débeurrer *v.* – to clean up, to wash up; typically used only for a person, in a literal sense.

Débile *adj., n.m.* – awesome, unbelievable, insane; can be used in a positive or negative sense.
C'est débile, ce film-là! – That film is just amazing!

Débiné(e) *adj.* – depressed, demotivated

Débiner *v.i.* – to depress, to demotivate
Sa copine l'a quitté, alors il est mal débiné. – His girlfriend left him, so he's pretty depressed.

Décâlissant(e)★ *adj.* – depressing, a downer

Décâlissé(e)★ *adj.* – 1. depressed, down, heartbroken (used for a person); 2. damaged, destroyed (used for an object)

Décâlisser★ *v.t.* – 1. to depart; 2. to depress

Décapant *n.m.* – Coca-Cola

Déconcrissé(e) *adj.* – in pieces, in ruins

Déconcrisser *v.t.* – to demolish, to destroy

Décrissant★ *adv.* – depressing, a downer

Décrissé(e)★ *adj.* – bummed out, disappointed, let down
Moi, j'étais vraiment décrissé après. – I was really bummed out afterwards.

Décrisser★ *v.i.* – 1. to beat it, to leave, to depart; 2. to damage, to ruin
Hé! Décrisse de là! – Hey! Get the heck outta here!

Décrivable *adj.* – describable, able to be explained

Ma situation n'est pas vraiment décrivable. – I can't really describe my situation.

Décrocher *v.* – 1. *Fr.* to stall, to lose momentum; 2. to fail, give up (particularly school)

Lui, il décroche encore de l'école. – He's failing in school again.

Décrocheur(euse) *n.m./f.* – (school) dropout

Dedans *prep.* – in, within

✻ *en dedans que* – in less than

Défaite *n.f.* – excuse, pretense

J'ai une défaite pour avoir manqué son partie. – I have an excuse for missing his party.

Définitivement *adv.* – definitely, certainly

Dégêné(e) *adj* – relaxed, at ease

(se) Dégêner – *v.t.* – to loosen up, to relax

(se) Dégreyer *v.i.* – 1. to take one's coat off, to get undressed; 2. to clear a table after a meal

Va te dégreyer et reste donc un peu. – Take your coat off and stay a while, then!

Veux-tu me dégreyer la table, s'il te plaît? – Would you clear the table for me, please?

Dégrincher *v.t.* – to destroy, to undo

(se) Dégripper *v.t.* – to get better, to heal up

(se) Déguédiner *v.i.* – to hurry up, to move quickly

Déjeuner *v.i.* – to have breakfast

Déjeuner *n.m.* – breakfast; in France, *petit-déjeuner* is usually used for breakfast, and *déjeuner* is used for lunch.

Démancher *v.t.* – to take off, remove, take down

De même *adv.* – like this/that
Je n'aime pas les gars de même. – I don't like guys like that.

(à) Demeure *adj.* – 1. well-built, well-contructed; 2. completely, totally

Demeurer *v.i.* – to live, to reside in
On demeure à Montréal en ce moment. – We live in Montreal at the moment.

(se) Déniaiser *v.i.* – to wise up, to smarten up

Dép. *contr.* "*dépanneur*" – convenience store
✳ *passer au dép.* – swing by the convenience store

Dépanneur *n.m.* – 1. convenience store; 2. *Fr.* towing company

Dépareillé(e) *adj.* – unique, remarkable

Dépasser *v.t.* – 1. to pass (such as in a car)
Il n'arrête jamais de dépasser des autos sur l'autoroute. – He never stops passing other cars on the highway.

Dépendamment *adv.* – depending on, as a function of (something)

Dépeinturer *v.t.* – to strip, to remove the paint from (something)
Il faut d'abord que je dépeinture le mur. – I have to strip the wall first.

Dépense *n.f.* – 1. cupboard, cabinet; 2. *Fr.* cost, expenditure
✳ *au diable la dépense* – to hell with the price (*lit.* to the devil with the price)

Dépensier(ère) *n.m./fem.* – spendthrift

De plus *adv.* – additionally, also

De quoi *pron.* – something
Je voudrais bien faire de quoi. – I'd really like to do something.

Déraincher *v.t.* – to destroy, to undo

Dérangeant(e) *adj.* – disturbing, bothersome

Dérencher *v.t.* – to pull (out), to dislocate
Ça c'est la troisième fois qu'il s'est dérenché le coudre. – This is the third time he'd dislocated his elbow.

Dérougir *v.i.* – to reduce, to diminish, to cease

(se) Désâmer *v.i.* – to work oneself to the bone, to give (a job or other task) one's all (*lit.* to de-soul oneself)
Ça fait quatre ans qu'il se désâme chez eux, sans aucun mot pour lui rémercier. – He's worked himself to the bone for four years there, without so much as a thank you.

Descendre *v., Fr.* – to descend, to go down
✹ *descendre tous les saints du ciel* – to swear (*lit.* to bring down all the saints from the heavens)

Désennui *n.m.* – pastime, diversion, hobby

Deshe*** *n.f.* – sperm, semen

Désouffler *v.t.* – to let the air out (of something)

De suite *adv.* – right away, immediately
On va faire ça de suite. – We'll do that right away.

Détail *n.m., Fr.* – detail, particular
✹ *à cheval sur les détails* – hung up on the details (*lit.* on horseback about the details)

Déteindu(e) *adj.* – faded, discolored (*lit.* un-tinted)

Dévirer *v.i.* – to turn aside, to change direction

Diable *n.m., Fr.* – devil
✹ *Le diable est aux vaches.* – used to describe a chaotic situation (*lit.* the devil is with the cows)
✹ *mener le diable* – to make a racket, cause a disturbance

✖ *tirer le diable par la queue* – to be very poor (*lit.* to pull the devil by the tail)

D'ici *conj.* – from now until
  d'ici un an – within a year

Différencer *v.t.* – to distinguish, to tell the difference between (things)
  Moi, je ne peux pas différencer les deux. – I can't tell the two apart.

faire du Diguidi ha ha *exp.* – 1. to screw around (joking sense); 2. to screw around (sexual sense)

Dîner *n.m.* – lunch

Dîner *v.i.* – to have lunch

Dire *v.t., Fr.* – to say
  ✖ *avoir pour son dire que* – to think that (*lit.* to have for his say that)

Disable *adj.* – something that can be said (*lit.* say-able)
  ✖ *c'est pas disable* – incredible, indescribable

Disconnecter *v.t.* – to disconnect, unplug

Discontinuer *v.t.* – to discontinue, stop producing

Dispendieux(euse) *adj., Fr.* – costly, expensive

Dix cennes *n.m.* – dime, 10-cent piece

Dix-huit roues *n.m.* – 18-wheeler (truck)

Dodicher *v.t.* – to cradle an infant (in one's arms)

Dompe *n.f.* – dump, waste disposal site

Domper *v.t.* – to throw out, to dump

Donner *v.* – 1. *Fr.* to give; 2. to seem, to appear (when speaking about the result of something)
  Ça donne le bon effet. – That yields the right effect.
  Ça donne un peu trop compliqué. – That seems a bit complicated.

✹ *donner la bascule* – traditional Quebec birthday practice of grabbing someone by the shoulders and ankles and tossing them into the air the same number of times as their age (*lit.* to give someone the see-saw).

✹ *donner la claque* – to give it your best
Donnes-y la claque! – Give it a try!

✹ *donner de la merde à (quelqu'un)*★ – to give (someone) shit

✹ *donner de la misère à (quelqu'un)* – to give (someone) a hard time

✹ *donner du slack à (quelqu'un)* – to give (someone) some slack

✹ *donner le diable à (quelqu'un)* – to give (someone) hell

✹ *donner son 4 %* – to send away, to fire; a reference to the standard four percent vacation pay in Quebec, typically reimbursed upon termination of employment.

✹ *donner un bec sur la suce* – to give someone a kiss on the lips

✹ *donner un lift* – to give (someone) a lift

Dorénavant *adv., Fr.* – henceforth, from this time on

Dormir *v.i., Fr.* – to sleep

✹ *dormir au gaz* – to waste time, to be slow (*lit.* to sleep on the gas)

✹ *dormir sur la switch* – to waste time, to be slow (*lit.* to sleep on the switch)

Dos *n.m., Fr.* – back, rear side

✹ *parler dans le dos de quelqu'un* – to talk behind someone's back

Douance *n.f.* – intelligence, qualities of a gifted person

Doudou *n.f.* – blanket, comforter

Douillette *n.f.* – blanket, comforter

Doux *adj., Fr.* – soft

✹ *doux comme un agneau* – very polite, very gentle; usually said of someone kind.

Down *n.m.* – period of depression or malcontentment
Après que mon chum m'a quittée, j'ai eu un gros down. – After my boyfriend left me, I was really down for a while.

Down *adj.* – down, depressed

Drap *n.m., Fr.* – sheet, curtain
 ✳ *être blanc comme un drap* – to be as white as a sheet

(à) Drette *n.m., def. "(à) droite"* – 1. (to the) right; 2. straight
 ✳ *drette à soir* – as of this evening
 ✳ *drette là* – right there
 ✳ *tout drette* – straight ahead

Driver *v.t.* – to be in charge of, to be in control of, to drive
 C'est toi qui vas driver ce projet? – You're the one who will drive this project?

Drôle *adj., Fr.* – 1. funny, amusing; 2. strange, weird
 ✳ *drôle d'affaire* – strange situation

Dropper *v.t.* – 1. to drop, to let go (of something); 2. to plummet downward
 Je vais le dropper, s'il continue de même. – I'll let him go if he continues like this.

Dû *adj.* – due, required
 ✳ *dû à* – due to
 ✳ *dû pour* – due for
 Mon char est dû pour un changement d'huile. – My car is due for an oil change.

Dull *adj.* – boring, dull
 ✳ *dull à mourir* – deathly boring

Dumper *v.t.* – 1. to throw away; 2. to drop (someone) off; 3. to break up with (someone)
 Ma blonde m'a dumpé il y a trois jours. – My girlfriend dumped me three days ago.

Dur(e) *adj., Fr.* – 1. hard; 2. difficult

  ❋ *faire dur* – 1. to be in a bad situation or state, to be rough; 2. to be idiotic, ridiculous, ugly, or crazy; 3. to be badly dressed

  Ça fait un peu dur. – That's kind of a difficult situation.

Durant que *conj.* – while, during

E

É *expr., def.* "*elle est*" – she is

Eau *n.f., Fr.* – water

- *avoir de l'eau dans la cave* – to wear pants that are too short (*lit* to have water in the basement)
- *être dans l'eau bouillante/chaude* – to be in hot water, to be in trouble
- *faire de l'argent comme de l'eau* – to make a lot of money (*lit.* to make money like water)
- *faire eau* – to leak (water)

Écartant(e) *adj.* – disorienting; typically used to describe an area in which it's easy to become lost.

Écarter *v.t.* – to lose (something)

J'ai écarté ma montre. – I lost my watch.

s'Écarter *v.i.* – to lose one's way, to become disoriented

Elle est pas mal écartée. – She's pretty lost.

Je m'écarte chaque fois que je marche dans ce coin-là. – I get lost every time I walk around that area.

Écartillé(e) *adj.* – with legs spread apart

Je l'ai trouvé tout écartillé dans la neige. – I found him spread-eagle in the snow.

Échapper *v.t.* – 1. *Fr.* to escape; 2. to drop, to let go

J'ai échappé mon crayon par terre. – I dropped my pen on the floor.

- *échapper une occasion* – to lose an opportunity

s'Échapper *v.i.* – 1. to be indiscreet; 2. to lose one's cool, to become angry

Échouer *v.t.* – to fail (a test, etc.)

Écœurant(e) *adj.* – 1. amazing, phenomenal, out of this world; 2. disgusting

C'est un film écœurant! – It's an amazing film!

Je trouvais son attitude écœurante. – I found his attitude to be disgusting.

Écœurer★ *v.t.* – to piss off, to bother, to annoy
Il m'a écœuré toute la nuit, ce gars-là. – That guy annoyed me the whole night.

École *n.f., Fr.* – school
   ✹ *école de rang* – country(side) school
   ✹ *foxer l'école* – to play hooky, to cut school

Écornifler *v.i.* – to snoop, to peep, to spy on

Écornifleur(euse) *n.m./fem.* – snooper, peeping tom

Écourtiché(e) *adj.* – very short (for clothes)

Écouter *v.t.* – 1. *Fr.* to listen; 2. to watch (a movie, television, etc.); 3. to obey, to pay attention to
Il faut que tu m'écoutes! – You have to listen to me!
   ✹ *écouter la musique à planche* – to listen to very loud music (*lit.* to listen to music flat-out)
   ✹ *écouter une vue* – to watch a movie
On a écouté un très bon film hier. – We watched a great film yesterday.

Écrapouti(e) *adj.* – crushed, collapsed

Écrapoutir *v.t.* – to collapse, to break down
   (s')Écraser – *v.t.* – to crash out, to relax
On s'est écrasé sur le divan. – We crashed out on the sofa.

Efface *n.f.* – eraser

Effoirer *v.t.* – to crush, to flatten

s'Effoirer *v.t.* – to crash (out), to collapse
Après la partie, on s'est effoirés chez lui. – After the party, we crashed at his place.

Effrayant *adj., Fr.* − 1. incredible, disturbing, terrible; 2. surprising, incredible, extraordinary

C'est effrayant comment qu'elle croit tout ce qu'il dit. − It's incredible how she believes everything he says.

Égal *adv.* − equally, in equal measure

✱ *partager (quelque chose) égal* − to split (something) equally

Égarouillé(e) *adj.* − wild, crazed

Il me regardait avec des yeux égarouillés. − He looked at me with wild eyes.

(s')Éjarrer *v.i.* − 1. to crash out, to spread out; 2. to attempt to do several things at once (without success)

En arrivant chez moi, j'ai trouvé mon fils éjarré dans le fauteuil. − Upon arriving home, I found my son crashed out on the sofa.

Embarquer *v.i.* − to get in, get on, join

On va tous embarquer sur le projet ensemble. − We're all going to join the project together.

✱ *embarquer quelqu'un sur le pouce* − to pick up someone hitchhiking

Veux-tu embarquer avec moi? − Do you want to ride (in the car) with me?

Embarré(e) *adj.* − locked in, closed in

Je me suis fait embarrer au bureau. − I got myself locked in the office.

(s')Emmieuter *v.i.* − to become nicer weather, to clear off

Selon lui, il devrait s'emmieuter après midi. − According to him, it should clear off after noon.

(s')Empironner *v.i.* − to become worse weather, to sock in

pour Emporter *v.t.* − to take out, to go

Je prendrais deux cafés pour emporter, s'il vous plaît. − I'd like two coffees to go, please.

En autant que *expr.* – insofar as

En bas de *prep.* – beneath

Encan *n.m.* – auction

(s')Endormir *v.t., Fr.* – 1. to go to sleep; 2. to be sleepy, to doze off
Je m'endormais derrière le volant. – I was asleep at the wheel.

Endurer *v.t.* – to put up with, to endure
Je ne peux plus l'endurer. – I can't stand him anymore.

Ènéoué *expr., def. Eng. "anyway"* – anyway, anyhow

(s')Énerver *v.i.* – to get upset
✱ *s'ennerver le poil des jambes* – to get upset (*lit.* to excite one's leg hair)

Enfarge *n.f.* – obstacle

(s')Enfarger *v.i.* – 1. to become tangled up in, to get stuck in (something); 2. to trip
✱ *s'enfarger dans les fleurs (du tapis)* – to become mired in the details (*lit.* to become caught up in the [carpet] flowers)

(se faire) Enfirouaper *v.* – to get led along, to get taken

Engagé(e) *adj.* – in use, taken
La ligne est engagée. – The line is busy.

Engraisser *v.i.* – to gain weight

Enlever *v., Fr.* – to remove, to take off
✱ *enlever une pelure* – to remove one's coat (*lit.* to take off a layer)

Enmieuter *v.i.* – to get better, to improve

Ennuyance *n.f.* – annoyance

Ennuyant(e) *adj.* – tiring, boring, annoying

Ennuyeux(euse) *adj.*, *Fr.* – tiring, boring, annoying

(c'est) En plein ça *expr.* – (that's) pretty much it, (that's) completely the case

Enregistreuse *n.f.* – tape recorder

Enteka *expr.*, *def.* "*en tout cas*" – anyhow, in any case

En tout temps que *expr.* – anytime that

Entre autres *adv.* – among other things

Envoye donc! *expr.* – C'mon, then!

Enwaille (donc)! *expr.*, *def.* "*envoye donc*" – C'mon! Move your butt!

Épais(se) *adj.*, *n. masc./fem.* – 1. thick-skulled (person); 2. fool, idiot, numskull
Ce gars là est un épais. – That guy is a numskull.

Épaisseur *adj.*, *n.m.*, *Fr.* – thickness
✸ *s'habiller en epaisseurs* – to dress in layers (*lit.* to dress in thicknesses)

Épaté(e) *adj.* – impressed

Épater *v.t.* – to impress
✸ *épater la gallerie* – to make a grand entrance

Épeurant(e) *adj.* – scary

Épeurer *v.t.* – to scare, frighten

Épicerie *n.f.* – grocery store
✸ *faire l'épicerie* – to go food shopping

Épinette *n.f.* – spruce (gum), used for its medicinal qualities (e.g., as a sedative, aid for digestion, etc.).
✸ *bière d'épinette* – spruce beer

Épingle *n.f.* – pin, holder
✸ *épingle à linge* – clothespin

Épinglette *n.f.* – brooch, pin

Épivarder *v.t.* - to reprimand, to scold

s'Épivarder *v.i.* – 1. to take a breather, to get out a bit; 2. to spread oneself too thin

Épluchette *n.f.* – corn-husking party, in which guests husk and cook corn as a part of the festivities.

Épouvant(e) *adj.* – incredible, unbelievable
    ✱ *àller à l'épouvant* – to go at full speed

Épouvantable *adj.* – atrocious

Épuisé(e) *adj., Fr.* – burned out, extremely tired

Escalier roulant *n.m.* – escalator

Escousse *n.f., def. "secousse"* – a while, a period of time

Espadrille *n.f.* – sneakers, sports shoes

Espérer *v.i.* – 1. *Fr.* to hope; 2. to wait for
    Espère-moi sur le coin, j'arrive. – Wait for me on the corner, I'll be right there.

Essence *n.f.* – flavour, taste, smell

Essuie-vitre *n.m.* – winshield wiper

Estimé *n.m.* – estimate, price quote

Étage *n.m., Fr.* – floor, stage; in Quebec, the first floor of a building is usually called *premier étage*, whereas in France it is more often called *rez-de-chaussée.*

Étampe *n.f.* – stamp, symbol

Étamper *v.t.*– to stamp

Été des Indiens: *expr.* – Indian summer

Être *v.* – to be

* *être à coté de la track* – to be in error, to make a mistake (*lit.* to be next to the [train] track)
* *être à main* – 1. to be friendly, obliging; 2. to be close, right at hand
* *être à pic* – to be grumpy, irritable
* *être à pied* – to be in financial difficulty; opposite sense from English "to be on one's feet" (to be financially independent).
* *être assis sur son steak* – to be in a comfortable financial position (*lit.* seated upon [one's] steak)
* *être au coton* – 1. to be at the end of one's means or patience; 2. to be exhausted
* *être aux femmes*– to be homosexual (for a woman)
* *être aux hommes* – to be homosexual (for a man)
* *être ben chum avec (quelqu'un)* – to be really chummy with (someone)
* *être (bien) blond* – to be dumb (*lit.* to be [very] blond)
* *être bien gréyé* – to be all set, to be ready
* *être bossu* – to be skilled in business
* *être capable (de)* – to be able (to do something)
* *être chaud* – to be drunk, to be lit
* *être dans la lune* – to be spaced out (*lit.* to be on the moon)
* *être dans l'eau bouillante/chaude* – to be in hot water, to be in trouble
* *être dans le champ* - to be in error, to be mistaken (*lit.* to be in the field)
* *être dans le jus* – to be swamped, to be busy (*lit.* to be in the juice)
* *être dans le rouge* – to be in the red, to be in financial difficulty
* *être dans le rush* – to be in a rush
* *être dans les patates* – to be in error, to be mistaken (*lit.* to be in the potatoes)
* *être dans le trou* – to be in trouble (*lit.* to be in the hole)
* *être d'avance* – to be positive, to be forward-looking

�># *être de bonne heure sur le piton* – to be up at the crack of dawn (*lit.* to be on the button early)
✳ *être de la petite bière* – to be without importance (*lit.* to be of small beer)
✳ *être en balloune* – to be pregnant
✳ *être en boisson* – to be drunk
✳ *être en crisse*★★ – to be pissed off, to be upset
✳ *être en (beau) joualvert* – to be furious
✳ *être en tabarnac*★★ – to be pissed off, to be upset
✳ *être game* – to be willing, to be game
✳ *être habillé comme la chienne à Jacques* – to be badly dressed (*lit.* to be dressed like Jacques's dog)
✳ *être ketchup* – 1. to be easy; 2. to be complete
✳ *(ne pas) être la fin du monde* – to (not) be the end of the world
✳ *être mieux de* – to be better to
✳ *être mort de rire* – 1. to be dying (of laughter); 2. to be all set, to be guaranteed success
✳ *être né pour un petit pain* – born to be mediocre (*lit.* to be born for a little bread)
✳ *être parlable* – to be able to be talked with
✳ *être pogné sur (quelqu'un)* – to be stuck on (someone)
✳ *être pour (quelque chose)* – to be in favour of (something), to be for (something)
✳ *être rond comme une bine* – to be completely sloshed/drunk (*lit.* to be as round as a bean)
✳ *être supposé de* – to be supposed to
✳ *être sur la brosse* – to be smashed, to be drunk (*lit.* to be on the brush)
✳ *être sur la décrisse*★ – to be wrecked, to be in a piteous state
✳ *être sur le BS (bien-être social)* – to be on welfare
✳ *être sur le partie* – to be in party-mode, to be on a bender
✳ *être tout croche* – to be bad, to be dirty, to be distasteful
• *être une bine* – to be nothing, to be small

Étrivant(e) *adj* – annoying, teasing

Étriver *v.t.* – to tease, to annoy, to perturb

Eux-autres *pron.* – they, them

(s')Evacher *v.i.* – to crash out, to relax

(s')Evader *v.i.* – to leave, to disappear

(s')Exciter *v.i., Fr.* – to become excited
   ✱ *s'exciter le poil des jambes* – to get upset (*lit.* to excite one's leg hair)

Excusez! *v.* – Excuse me!

Extensionner *v.t.* – to prolong, to extend
   J'ai fait réparer mon moteur, ça va extensionner un peu combien (de temps) ça dure. – I just had my motor fixed, which should make it last a bit longer.

F

Face *n.f., Fr.* – face, front
- ✱ *avoir la face à terre* – to be annoyed, to be vexed
- ✱ *avoir un face de bœuf* – to be in a bad mood (*lit.* to have a face of an ox)
- ✱ *une face à fesser dédans* – a hateful face

Fâchant(e) *adj.* – irritating, annoying, bothersome

Facture *n.m.* – bill, tab (*lit.* invoice)

Fafoin(e) *adj.* – idiot, fool (for a person)
- ✱ *faire en fafoin* – to screw up, to do badly

Faire *v., Fr.* – 1. to do, to make; 2. to seem, to appear
- ✱ *Ça fait!* – That'll do!
- ✱ *Ça va faire.* – That will do. That's enough.
- ✱ *(se) faire amancher* – to be had, to be taken advantage of
- ✱ *faire ami (avec quelqu'un)* – to become friends (with someone)
- ✱ *faire à mitaine* – to do by hand (*lit.* to do by mitten)
- ✱ *faire application* – to apply (*ex.* for a job)
- ✱ *faire attention à* – take care of
- ✱ *faire chier* – to suck, to be bad
- ✱ *faire coton* – to be pathetic
- ✱ *faire danser les dentiers* – to knock someone's lights out (*lit.* to make someone's teeth dance)
- ✱ *faire de la broue* – to blow hot air, to talk big (*lit.* to make suds)
- ✱ *faire de l'argent comme de l'eau* – to make a lot of money (*lit.* to make money like water)
- ✱ *faire des accroires* – to make (someone) believe something untrue, to deceive someone
- ✱ *faire des yeux de porc frais* – to be wide-eyed (*lit.* make fresh pork eyes)
- ✱ *faire du barda* – to be noisy
- ✱ *faire du (bon) sens* – to make (good) sense

❋ *faire du diguidi ha ha* – 1. to screw around (joking sense); 2. to screw around (sexual sense)

❋ *faire du pouce* – to hitchhike

❋ *faire dur* – 1. to be in a bad situation or state, to be rough; 2. to be idiotic, ridiculous, ugly, or crazy; 3. to be badly dressed

❋ *faire du snow* – to snowboard

❋ *faire du temps* – to do time (in prison)

❋ *faire eau* – to leak (water)

❋ *faire en fafoin* – to screw up, to do badly

❋ *(se) faire enfirouaper* – to get screwed over, to get taken

❋ *faire faire (quelque chose)* – to have (something) done

Je vais le faire faire. – I'm going to have it done.

Je vais t'en faire faire! – I'm going to do you in!

❋ *faire fitter* – to adjust

❋ *faire la baboune* – to pout

❋ *faire la commande* – to go (food) shopping

❋ *faire l'affaire* – to be sufficient, to do the job

❋ *faire la galette* – to make (a lot of) money

❋ *faire la palette* – to make a lot of money

❋ *faire le bec fin* – to be fussy about what one eats

❋ *faire le drôle* - to clown around

❋ *faire le gros bec* – to pout (*lit.* to make a big face)

❋ *faire le motton* – to make bucks, to make money

faire le piastre – to make bucks, to make a lot of money

❋ *faire l'épicerie* – to go food shopping

❋ *faire les cent pas* – to pace (back and forth) (*lit.* to do the hundred paces)

❋ *(se) faire mettre*** – to get laid, to have sex (with someone)

❋ *faire mononcle* – to be old-fashioned, to seem old-fashioned

❋ *(se) faire monter les oreilles* – to get a haircut (*lit.* to get one's ears lifted)

❋ *faire opérer* – to make (something) function, to make (something) work

❋ *faire patate* – to fail (*lit.* to make potatoes)

❋ *faire patienter* – to make (someone) wait

✱ *(se) faire pleumer* – to get taken, to be had (*lit.* to get plucked)

✱ *(se) faire rentrer dedans* – 1. to be hit (by a vehicle or object); 2. to be scolded or otherwise verbally berated

✱ *faire sa bosse* – to make a bundle (of money) (*lit.* to make one's bump)

✱ *faire semblant* – to pretend

✱ *faire son smatte* – to show off

✱ *faire (son) rapport à (quelqu'un)* – to (make one's) report to (someone)

✱ *(se) faire taper les foufounes* – to get a spanking

✱ *faire tata* – to wave goodbye

✱ *Fais-toi-s'en pas.* – Don't worry about it

✱ *faire un air bête* – to look (at someone) with contempt

✱ *faire un boute* – to blow out of somewhere, to leave, to depart

✱ *faire un canular* – to set up a (hidden) candid camera

✱ *faire une saucette* – to go for a dip (in a pool, etc.)

✱ *faire un pli* – to be bothered or upset by something

✱ *faire un téléphone* – to place a call

✱ *se faire aller* – to hurry up

Ay, fais-toi aller, la réunion commence dans trois minutes. – Hurry it up, the meeting starts in three minutes!

✱ *se faire avoir* – to be had, to be taken advantage of

✱ *se faire botter le cul** – to get kicked in the ass

✱ *se faire bumper* – to get bumped out, to be pushed aside

✱ *se faire emplir* – to be screwed over, to be taken advantage of (by a person or situation)

(se) Faire à croire *v.i.* – to make believe, to pretend

Faisable *adj.* – possible, doable

✱ *être faisable* – to be doable

Fait(e) *adj.* – 1. done, complete; 2. done in, in trouble

Il est fait, là. – He's really in trouble now.

✱ *fait à l'os* – completely finished, completely done (*lit.* done to the bone)

(ça) Fait que *expr.* – so, that's why

Il était fatigué, fait qu'on est rentré plus tôt. – He was tired, so we went home early.

Faker *v.t.* – to fake, to pretend

Falle *n.f.* – throat, chest

✱ *avoir la falle basse* – to have a long face, to be down

Fantasmer *v.i.* – to dream (of something)

Faque *expr., contr. "fait que"* – so, that's why

Farce *n.f.* – joke

C'est pas des farces! – It's not a joke!

Fardouches *n.f. pl.* – underbrush, undergrowth

Fauché: *adj.* – broke, out of money

Fendant(e): *n.m./fem., adj.* – pretentious, arrogant (person)

Fermer: *v., Fr.* – to close, to shut

✱ *fermer (un endroit)* – to close (a place, such as a bar)

Il est déjà 2 h 45, on va fermer la place! – It's already 2:45 a.m., we're going to close the place!

✱ *Ferme ta soue!* – Shut your trap! (*lit.* Shut your sty!)

Fesse: *n.f.* – butt, rear-end, hindquarters

✱ *jouer au fesses*★ – to screw, to have sex with (someone)

Fesser *v.i.* – 1. to strike, to hit headfirst; 2. to have a kick, to be strong; often used to describe a beverage, etc.

Aye, ça fesse, ta boisson! – Hey, your drink really has a kick!

✱ *(une) face à fesser dédans* – a hateful face

✱ *fesser dans le dash* – to be surprising, to be unexpected

Lui, il a fessé dans le mur. – He bashed (headfirst) into the wall.

Fête *n.f.* – 1. *Fr.* party; 2. birthday

Fête de la Reine *n.f.* – Victoria Day (named after Queen Victoria)

Fête du Travail *n.f* – Labour day

Fève *n.f., Fr.* – bean
> ❋ *fèves au lard* – baked beans

Feu *n.m., Fr.* – fire.
> ❋ *avoir le feu au cul*★ – to be furious (*lit.* to have fire in the ass)
> ❋ *avoir le feu au passage*★ – to be furious (*lit.* to have fire in the passage)
> ❋ *mouche à feu* – lightning bug, firefly
> ❋ *vente de feu* – fire sale

Fier-pet *adj., n.m./fem.* – proud, vain

Fif/Fifi *n.m., adj.* – 1. homosexual (in attitude or action), only used in the masculine; 2. fraidy-cat, chicken

Filer *v.* – to feel (well)
Non, je file pas bien, là. – No, I don't feel very well right now.

Filière *n.f.* – filing cabinet

Film de cul *expr.* – porno film

Fin(e) *adj.* – kind, sweet, likeable, gentle, nice, generous
Il est tellement fin, ce gars-là! – He's such a great guy!

Fin *n.f., Fr.* – end
> ❋ *fin de semaine* – weekend
> ❋ *fin de soirée* – (rest of) the evening
> *Bonne fin de soirée!* – Have a good evening!

Finissant(e): *n.m./f.* – graduating student
> ❋ *Album des finissants* – yearbook

Fitter *v.t.* – to fit, to go (together)
Attends, je vais le faire fitter un peu mieux. – Hold on, I'm going to adjust it a bit further.

Tout ça ne pourrait jamais fitter ensemble. − All that could never go together.

✷ *faire fitter* − to adjust

Flagger *v.t.* - to hail, to flag (down)

✷ *flagger un taxi* − to hail a cab

Flagosse *n.f.* − small problem or issue

Flagosser *v.i.* − to waste time, to do unimportant things

Flanc-mou(molle) *adj., n.m./fem.* − lazy (person)

✷ *grand flanc-mou* − good-for-nothing

Flancher *v.i., Fr.* − to fail, to go out of service

Flash *n.m.* − idea, thought

Je viens d'avoir un flash. − I just had a thought.

Flasher *v.i.* − to occur to (someone)

Juste après, l'idée m'a flashé. − Just afterwards, the idea occurred to me.

Flopper *v.i.* − to fail, to flop

Flot *n.m./f.* − child

Oui, on a des flots à la maison. − Yes, we have kids at home.

Flusher *v.t.* − 1. to flush (a toilet); 2. to break up with or drop (a relationship); 3. to fire

Ils sortent plus ensemble. Elle l'a flushé il y a trois jours. − They're not going out any more. She dumped him three days ago.

Flux *n.m* − diarrhea

Flyé(e) *adj.* − extravagant, extreme, fly; generally used to describe a person.

Focusser (sur) *v.i.* − to focus (on)

Foin *n.m.* − money

Foirer *v.i.* – 1. to party, to have fun; 2. to tank, to fail
Ça va foirer complètement après. – That's going to completely tank afterwards.

Folie furieuse *n.f.* – mad panic
C'était la folie furieuse au bureau pour le quart d'heure avant son arrivé. – It was a mad panic in the office for the fifteen minutes before he arrived.

Follerie *n.f.* – silliness, crazy thing
J'ai fait une follerie. J'ai acheté une bouteille de Château d'Yquem pour son anniversaire! – I did something silly. I bought him a bottle of Château d'Yquem for his birthday.

Forçant(e) *adj.* – difficult, requiring force

Formule-1 *adj., n.f.* – the best, top-notch; reference to the annual Formula-1 race held in Montreal.

Fort(e) *adj., Fr.* – strong
✱ *boire du fort* – to drink alcohol (*lit.* to drink some strong [stuff])

Fortiller *v.i.* – to move non-stop, to twitch

Fou(Folle) *adj., Fr.* – crazy, insane
✱ *fou bracque* – completely nuts
✱ *fou raide* – completely nuts

Foufounes★ *n.f.* – butt, backside, rear-end
✱ *(se) faire taper les foufounes* – to get a spanking

Fouille *n.m.* – fall, spill
✱ *prendre une fouille* – to take a fall

Fouler *v.i.* – to shrink, to pull back

Fournaise *n.m.* – furnace, heating system

Fourneau *n.m.* – oven

Fourrant(e) *adj.* – confusing, annoying, inconvenient, bad

Fourré(e) *adj.* – confused, screwed-up

(se) Fourrer*** *v.* – 1. to screw up, to err; 2. to screw (sexual sense)
✱ *fourrer le chien* – to mess things up (*lit.* to screw the dog)
Je me suis fourré avec cette affaire-là. – I screwed myself with that deal.

Foxer *v.t.* – to cheat, to abscond
✱ *foxer l'école* – to play hooky, to cut school
✱ *foxer un cours* – to skip a class

appel à Frais virés *exp.* – collect call

Franchement *expr.* – really

Frapper *v., Fr.* – to hit, to strike
✱ *frapper dans le beurre* – to blow it, to miss one's chance
✱ *frapper un nœud* - to hit a wall, to encounter a significant obstacle

Freaker *v.i.* – to freak (out), to panic
L'affaire m'a fait freaker pendant au moins une semaine. – The whole deal freaked me out for at least a week.

Frencher *v.* – to tongue/french kiss

Frette *adj., def. "froid"* – cold
✱ *péter au frette* – to drop dead (*lit.* to stop cold)

(une) Frette *n.f.* – cold, referring to beer (*sim.* a cold one)
On va aller se boire une frette – We're gonna go drink a cold one

Frigidaire *n.m.* – refrigerator

Friler *v.i.* – to shiver, to tremble (with cold, etc.)

Frileux(euse) *adj.* – quick to be cold; generally said of a person
Ma blonde est vraiment frileuse. – My girlfriend gets cold really quickly.

Fripé(e) *adj.* – wiped out, wasted
À cause de la partie, j'étais tout fripé le lendemain. – Because of the party, I was pretty wiped out the next morning.

Friper *v.i.* – to waste

Friperie *n.f.* – second-hand (clothing) store

Froque *n.f.* – coat

Frosté(e) *adj.* – wiped out, out of it

Après avoir passé toute la nuit au travail, j'étais pas mal frosté. – After spending all night at work, I was pretty zoned out.

Fru(e) *adj., contr. "frustré"* – frustrated

Frustré(e) *adj., Fr.* – upset, frustrated, annoyed

Frustrer *v.i., Fr.* – to upset, to frustrate, to annoy

Ça me frustre un peu de ne pas pouvoir y aller. – It frustrates me a bit not to be able to go.

Fucké(e)★★ *adj.* – screwed up, fucked up; a less vulgar and visceral sense than in English.

✱ *fucké au boutte* – completely screwed up

La situation est fuckée au boutte. – The situation is completely screwed up.

✱ *fucké ben raide★★* – completely screwed up (*lit.* screwed good and stiff)

✱ *fucké dans la tête* – screwed up in the head, messed up

Fucker★★ *v.t.* – to screw up, to fuck up

✱ *fucker le chien* – 1. to screw around; 2. to have difficulty doing something

Fuck friend★ *n.m.* – lover, casual sex partner

Fuck off★★ *expr.* – screw it,, the hell with it, then; not generally a comment directed at a person, but instead the dismissal of a situation or intent.

✱ *Il y a trop de monde. Fuck off, on reviendra demain.* – There're too many people. Screw it, let's come back tomorrow.

Full *adj., adv.* – completely, very, fully

Maman, le frigo est full vide! – Mom, the fridge is completely empty!

✱ *à full pine* – at full speed

Moi, j'ai full d'affaires à faire. – I have lots of work to do.

Fun *n.m.* – fun, enjoyment

Hé! c'est le fun, ça! – Hey, that's cool!

✱ *avoir du fun* – to have fun, to have a good time.

On va avoir du fun demain. – We're going to have a good time tomorrow.

✱ *un fun noir* – a crazy good time

✱ *pour le fun* – for the fun of it, not serious

Je ne voulais pas vraiment leur deranger. C'était juste pour le fun. – I didn't really mean to bother them. It was just for the fun of it.

Funérailles *n.f. pl.* – funeral

G

Galerie *n.f.* – balcony, terrace

Galette *n.f.. Fr.* – biscuit, small cake-like pastry
  ✱ *faire la galette* – to make (a lot of) money

Galon *n.m.* – measuring tape

Galvaude *n.f.* – poutine (french fries and cheese curds covered in gravy) mixed with chicken and peas.

Galvauder *v.i.* – 1. to tease, to flirt, to pursue the opposite sex; 2. to botch a job

Galvaudeux(euse) *n.m./fem.* – one who gallantly pursues the opposite sex

Game *adj* – willing, prepared
  ✱ *être game* – to be game, to be willing

Gant *n.m.* – glove
  ✱ *laisser tomber les gants* – to take the gloves off (*lit.* to forget about the gloves)
  ✱ *mettre des gants blancs* – to handle with kid gloves, to treat gently

Garde *v., contr. "regarder" in the imperative tense* – look
  Garde, je n'ai plus le temps pour ça. – Look, I don't have time for this anymore.
  ✱ *Garde donc!* – Look at that!

Garde-robe *n.m.* – closet, wardrobe
  ✱ *sortir du garde-robe* – to come out of the closet, to reveal one's homosexuality

Garderie *n.f., Fr.* – daycare centre

Gardien(ne) *n.masc./fem., Fr.* – babysitter

Gardon *expr., def.* *"regarde, donc"* – look, then
    Gardon, il faut que je te parles! – Look, I gotta talk with you.
    ✱ *Gardon ça!* – Check that out!

Garnotte *n.f.* – 1. pebble; 2. gravel

Garnotter *v.t.* – to whip or throw something (at something/someone)

Garrocher *v.t.* – 1. to toss, throw, or project something; 2. to work quickly or carelessly
    Les enfants garrochaient des roches au chien. – The children threw rocks at the dog.

Gars *n.m., Fr.* – guy; used in the possessive (*mon gars*) to add emphasis when speaking with someone, in somewhat the same sense as "dude" or "man" in English.
    Là, mon gars, j'étais complètement crevé. – At that point, dude, I was totally exhausted.

Gaspille *n.m.* – waste

Gâté(e) *adj.* – spoiled

Gâter *v.i.* – to spoil (someone)

Gaz *n.m, Fr.* – gas, fuel

Gazer *v.t.* – to fill up (with gas)

Gelé(e) *adj.* – 1. *Fr.* frozen; 2. stoned, baked (from drugs)

Geler *v.i.* – to be freezing, to be cold
    Moi, je gèle, là. – Well, I'm freezing.

Gênant(e) *adj., Fr.* – intimidating, blocking, causing hesitation
    Je trouvais son attitude un peu gênante. – I found his attitude somewhat intimidating.

Gêné(e) *adj.* – shy, hesitant, nervous
    Je suis gêné de parler à mon patron à ce sujet. – I'm hesitant to talk with my boss about that.

Gérant(e) *n.m. /f.* – manager

Genre *n.m., expr.* – 1. *Fr.* kind of, type; 2. like; the latter usage is almost identical to the slang American use of the word "like" in casual speech.
> *C'est est un gars cool, genre.* – He's, like, a cool guy.
> *C'est le genre de gars qui ferait ça.* – He's the kind of guy who'd do that.

Gicleur *n.m.* – fire sprinkler

Gigoter *v.i.* – to hurry up, to move quickly

Gilet *n.m.* – light shirt (especially a sports shirt)

Gîte (touristique) *n.m.* – bed & breakfast (B&B)

Gizmut: *n.m.* – gizmo

Glace *n.f.* – ice cube

Glandouneux(euse) *adj., n.m. /fem.* – lazy oaf, do-nothing, slacker

Gnochon(ne) *adj., n.m. /f.* – ignoramus, uneducated (person)

Goaler *v.i.* – 1. to act as a goalie (soccer); 2. to work very hard

Goaleur *n.m.* – goalie

Gogosse *n.f.* – small (cheap or unimportant) object

Gomme *n.f.* – 1. *Fr.* pencil eraser; 2. chewing gum

Gossage *n.m.* – fooling around, a waste of time

Gosse de robot *n.m.* – teaball

Gosser *v.i.* – 1. to fiddle with, to fool with (something); 2. to waste time on the details. 3. to bug, to bother

Gosses★ *n.m. /f.* – 1. *Fr.* children; 2. testicles
> ★ *avoir des gosses★* – to have balls, to be brave
> ★ *partir sur une gosse★* – to leave (somewhere) quickly (*lit.* to leave on a testicle)

Gosseux(euse) *adj., n.m./fem.* – 1. someone who likes to fiddle around with things; 2. a big talker, one who thinks him/herself bigger than their breeches

Gougounes *n.f.* – beach sandals, flip-flops

Goût *n.m., Fr.* – taste
> ✱ *avoir le goût (de faire quelque chose)* – to feel like (doing something)
> *J'ai le goût de faire l'amour.* – I feel like making love.

Grafigne *n.f.* – scratch

Grafigner *v.t.* – 1. to scratch, to graze; 2. to mar, to damage
Il s'est fait grafigner par son frère. – He was scratched by his brother.
S'il continue de même, ça va grafigner ma réputation. – If he continues this way, it will hurt my reputation.

Graine★★ *n.f.* – 1. schlong, penis; 2. idiot, fool

Graisser *v.t.* – to grease (up), to butter, typically used in cooking

Graisseuse *n.f.* – (an) order of french fries (*lit.* a greasy)

Grand monde *expr.* – high society, the upper crust

Grano *n.m., contr.* "*granola*" – granola

Grano(e) *adj.* – earthy, homey (usually said of a person)

Granola *n.m.* – health food fanatic

Gras dur: *expr.* – lucky (*lit.* hard fat)

Grassette *adj.f.* – chubby, overweight (used for a girl or woman)
Son visage est beau, mais elle est toutefois un peu grassette. – She's visually pretty, but a little chunky even so.

Grassouillette *adj.f.* – chubby, overweight (used for a girl or woman)

Gratin *n.m.* – the who's who, the upper crust

Le gratin artistique est venu cette soirée-là. – The who's who of the art world came that evening.

Gratte *n.f.* – 1. snowplow; 2. hand-held ice scraper

T'es malchanceux, mon homme, la gratte a déjà passé. –You're out of luck, my friend, the snowplow already went by.

Gratte-la-cenne *n.m.* – miser (*lit.* cent-scraper)

Gratter *v.i.* – to be stingy, to be tight-fisted

Gratteux(euse) *n.m./f., adj.* – (one who is) avaricious, stingy, or tight-fisted

Gratteux *n.m.* – scratchable lottery, ticket

Gravel *n.f.* – gravel

Gréluche *n.f.* – low-class or unintelligent woman

Gréyé(e) *adj.* – prepared, equipped, ready

✱ *être bien gréyé* – to be all set, to be ready

(se) Gréyer *v.i.* – to prepare, to equip oneself

Griller *v.t.* – to tan, to bake in the sun

Grippe *n.f., Fr.* – the flu

Grippé(e) *adj., Fr.* – infected with the flu

Gripette *adj.* – crabby, cranky

T'es pas mal gripette avant ton café le matin! – You're pretty cranky before your coffee in the morning!

Gros(se) *adj., Fr.* – large, big

✱ *gros comme un baril* – obese

✱ *gros comme une allumette* – as thin as a matchstick

Grosse Mol *expr.* – a large Molson beer

(se) Grouiller *v.i.* – to hurry up, to move quickly

Gruau *n.m.* – oatmeal, hot cereal

Guedaille *n.f.* – over-dressed, over-made woman

Guedille *n.f.* – 1. hot dog with sauerkraut; 2. snot
   ✱ *avoir la guedille au nez* – to have a runny nose

Guenille *n.f.* – 1. rag; 2. *n.f. pl.* (cheap) clothes
   ✱ *à chaque guenille son torchon* – to every girl her guy (*lit.* to each cloth its rag)

Gueule★ *n.f., Fr.* – 1. maw, mouth (of an animal); 2. a person's mouth or the words that come out of it.
   ✱ *avoir la gueule fendue jusqu'aux oreilles* – to be grinning from ear to ear

Gugus *n.m.* – small (cheap or unimportant) object

Guidoune★★ *n.f.* – whore, slut

H

Hab *n.m., contr.* "*habitant*" – redneck, country bumpkin

Habiller *v.t.* – to dress
* *être habillé comme la chienne à Jacques* – to be badly dressed (*lit.* to be dressed like Jacques's dog)
* *s'habiller en épaisseurs* – to dress in layers (*lit.* to dress in thicknesses)
* *s'habiller en pelures d'oignons* – to dress in layers (*lit.* to dress in onion skins)

Habit *n.m.* – suit of clothes
Je lui ai acheté un bel habit pour Noël. – I bought him a nice suit of clothes for Christmas.

Habitant(e)★ *adj., n.m./f.* – redneck, country bumpkin

Hambourgeois *n.m.* – hamburger

Haut *adj., Fr.* – high
* *en haut de* – above

Hein? *expr.* – What?

Herbe à puce *n.f.* – poison ivy

Heure *n.f., Fr.* – hour
* *heures d'affaires* – business hours

Hèvé *adj., def. Eng.* "*heavy*" – difficult, serious; the Québécois usage is generally restricted to descriptions of a weighty or serious situation.
La situation de sa mère est assez hèvée. – Her mother's situation is pretty serious.

Historique *n.f.* – story, tale
C'est une historique assez intéressante. – It's a pretty interesting story.

Hiver *n.m., Fr.* – winter

✱ *Qu'est-ce que ça mange en hiver?* – What is it like? (*lit.* What does it eat in winter?)

Homme *n. masc, Fr.* – man; often used in the possessive (*mon homme*) to add emphasis when speaking with someone, in somewhat the same sense as "dude" or "man" in English.

Là, mon homme, j'étais complètement crevé. – At that point, dude, I was totally exhausted.

Horaire *n.m.* – schedule, timetable

Veux-tu me vérifier l'horaire? – Would you check the schedule for me?

Hostic★ *see* ostic

Hostie★★ *see* ostie

Hot *adj.* – high-quality, neat, hot

Il est hot, ton char! – Your car is really hot!

Huard *n.m.* – dollar

Huile *n.f., Fr.* – oil

✱ *baigner dans l'huile* – to go smoothly, to be working okay (*lit.* to bathe in oil)

Quant au reste du projet, pour le moment ça baigne dans l'huile. – As for the rest of the project, for the moment it's going pretty smoothly.

✱ *huile à bras* –_elbow-grease, real effort

I

Ici *adv., Fr.* – here, in this place
  ✱ *D'ici* – between now and
  D'ici un an, il sera fait. – Within a year, it will be done.

Icitte *adv., def. "ici"* – here

Idée *n.f., Fr.* – idea
  ✱ *avoir toute son idée* – to be clear-minded; often said of an
  elderly person who is in full command of their senses.

Il n'y a pas de trouble! *expr.* – No worries!

Impassable *adj.* – unable to be traversed, blocked
  Après la tempête de verglas, ma rue était impassable pour la moitié
  d'une semaine. – After the ice storm, my road was blocked off for
  half a week.

Incontournable *adj.* – unforseeable, unavoidable

Inécoutable *adj.* – unlistenable

Innocenterie *n.f.* – silliness, stupidity

à l'Instant *n.m.* – right now, at the moment
  Il faut que tu le fasses à l'instant où je te le dis. – You need to do it
  precisely when I tell you.
  Il n'est pas parlable à l'instant. – You can't really talk with him
  right now.

Instantané(e) *adj.* – dissolvable powder form (such as coffee, soup, etc.)

Intéressant(e) *adj.* – 1. *Fr.* (intellectually) interesting, stimulating; 2.
important, a good thing
  C'est une histoire intéressante! – That's an interesting story!
  Paul ne vient pas, donc ça serait intéressant que tu viennes avec nous.
  – Paul isn't coming, so it would be a good thing if you came
  with us.

Intraduisible *adj.* – unable to be translated

Introduire *v.i., Fr.* – to introduce, present; Québécois often use this word (rather than *présenter*) for personal introductions.

Itinérant(e) *n.m./f., adj.* – homeless (person)

Itou *adv.* – also

J

Jack *n.m.* – Jack
- ✷ *bon Jack* – a good guy
- ✷ *grand Jack* – a big guy

Jacker *v.t.* – to jack up, to elevate

Jamb *n.f., Fr.* – leg
- ✷ *s'exciter le poil des jambes* – to get upset (*lit.* to excite one's leg hair)

Jambon *n.m., Fr.* – ham, hamhock
- ✷ *un gros jambon* – a self-satisfied individual

Jammé(e) *adj.* – stuck, jammed

Jammer *v.t.* – 1. to jam, to force; 2. to jam, to play music improvisationally

Jaquette *n.f.* – nightshirt

Jarnigoine *n.m./f.* – 1. chatterbox, talkative person; 2. intelligence, initiative
- ✷ *avoir le jarnigoine* – to be intelligent

Jaser *v.i.* – to chat with, to speak with (someone)
Ouais, on a jasé hier. – Yeah, we spoke yesterday.

Jasette *n.f.* – chat, quick conversation
- ✷ *piquer une jasette* – to have a chat

Jaspiner *v.i.* – to complain constantly, to lament

Jaspineux(euse) *adj., n.m./fem.* – one who complains constantly

Jériboire!★ *expr.* – Heck! Darn it!

Jésus-Christ!★ *expl.* – Jesus Christ!

Job *n.f.* – job, work
- ✷ *ajouter de la job* – to add work (to something)
- ✷ *job de bras* – grunt-work, labour (*lit.* arm-work)

Jos★★ *masc. pl.* – breasts

Joual *n.m.* – popular language, slang

Joualvert★ *expr.* – hell
 ✸ *être en (beau) joualvert*★ – to be furious

Jouer *v., Fr.* – to play
 ✸ *jouer au fesses*★ – to screw, to have sex with (someone)
 ✸ *jouer aux quilles* – to bowl, to go bowling

Joues *n.m. pl.* – affectionate term for a woman's behind (*lit.* cheeks)

Journée *n.f., Fr.* – day
 ✸ *avoir sa journée dans le corps* – to have had a rough day (*lit.* to have one's day in the body)
 ✸ *journée off* – vacation day

Jus *n.m.* – 1. juice; 2. sauce, stew; 3. electricity, current
 ✸ *être dans le jus* – to be swamped, to be busy (*lit.* to be in the sauce)

Juste *adj.* – 1. *Fr.* just, right (ethical sense); 2. close to, on the verge of something
 C'est juste un peu trop petit. – It's just a little too small.
 C'était juste! – He just made it!
 ✸ *au juste (adv.)* – actually

K

Kaline *expl., def.* *"câlisse"* – dammit

Kessé ça? *expr., contr.* *"Qu'est-ce que c'est, ça"* – What is that?

Kétaine *adj.* – taseless, bad
* *kétaine au boutte* – completely tasteless
Ses vêtements sont kétaines au boutte. – His clothes are completely tasteless.

Ketchup *adj., n.m.* – ketchup
* *être ketchup* – 1. to be easy; 2. to be complete

Kick *n.m.* – kick, blow
* *avoir un kick sur (quelqu'un)* – to have a crush on (someone)

Kicker *v.t.* – 1. to kick, propel forward; 2. to complain

Kif-kif *adj.* – an equal split, half and half

Kioute *adj.* – cute

Kodak *n.m.* – camera

Kossé? *expr., def.* *"Qu'est-ce que c'est?"* – What is it?

L

Là *adv., intej.* – 1. *Fr.* there, in that place; 2. now
> ✳ *Là, là* – now about that

Lâche *adj., Fr.* – lazy, laxidasical
> ✳ *lâche comme un âne* – as lazy as an ass (donkey)

Lâcher *v.* – 1. to quit, to give up, to let go; 2. to fail, to give out
Mon cellulaire va lâcher bientôt – My cellphone is going to give out pretty soon.
> ✳ *(se) lâcher lousse* – to let oneself loose, to have fun
> ✳ *Lâche pas la patate!* – Don't give up! (*lit.* Don't let go of the potato!)
> ✳ *lâcher son fou* – to let one's hair down, to let loose
> ✳ *lâcher un coup de fil* – to give someone a phone call
> ✳ *lâcher une fiouse* – to fart, to pass wind (*lit.* to pop a fuse)
> ✳ *lâcher un pet* – to fart, to pass wind
> ✳ *lâcher un wack* – to let out a yell

Là-dessus *conj.* – about it, about that
Je vais mettre un homme là-dessus. – I'll put a man on it.
Je voudrais bien te parler là–dessus. – I'd like to talk with you about that.

Laisser tomber *v, Fr.* – to drop something, to forget about something, to let (something) fall
> ✳ *laisser tomber les gants* – to take the gloves off (*lit.* to drop the gloves)

Lambineux(euse) *n.m./fem., adj.* – one who is indecisive or hesitant

Lancer *v.t., Fr.* – to throw, to launch (something)
> ✳ *lancer un ballon* – to start a rumour, particularly a political one

Langue *n.f., Fr.* – 1. tongue; 2. language, spoken tongue
> ✳ *avoir la langue à terre* – 1. to be exhausted; 2. to be very hungry (*lit.* to have one's tongue on the ground)

- *avoir la langue sale* – to have a dirty mouth (*lit.* to have a dirty tongue)
- *sur le bout de la langue* – on the tip of one's tongue

Lavage *n.m.* – laundry
J'ai tellement de lavage à faire! – I have so much laundry to do!

Lave-auto *n.m.* – car wash

Laveuse *n.f.* – washing machine

Légume *n.m., Fr.* – vegetable

- *le gros légume* – the big cheese, the important person (*lit.* the big vegetable)

Lendemain de veille *expr.* – the morning after the night before (after a party, etc.)

Lettres carrées *n.m. pl.* – capital letters (*lit.* square letters)

Lettres moulées *n.m. pl.* – capital (block) letters

Levée de fonds *expr.* – fundraising

Lever *v., Fr.* – 1. to lift, to raise; 2. to get out of bed

- *se lever du pied gauche* – to get up on the wrong side of the bed, to be cranky (*lit.* to get up on the left foot)
- *se lever le coude* – to have several beers (*lit.* to lift one's elbow)
- *se lever le gros orteil au nord* – to get up on the wrong side of the bed, to be cranky (*lit.* to get up with one's big toe pointed north)

Libre-service *n.m.* – self-service

Licencié(e) *adj.* – licence-holder, generally of a liquor licence; restaurants in Quebec often display the sign *"licence complete"* to indicate they sell alcohol.

Lichette *n.f.* – hickey, red mark left on the skin from a kiss

Licheux(euse): *adj., n.m./f.* – ass-kisser, brown-noser

Lift *n.m.* − ride, lift (in a vehicle)
- ✹ *donner un lift* − to give (someone) a lift
- ✹ *quêteux de lift* − one who incessently seeks out free rides

Ligne *n.f., Fr.* − 1. line up, waiting line; 2. phone line.
- ✹ *en bout de ligne* − ultimately, finally (*lit.* at the end of the line)

Limonade *n.f.* − lemonade

Linge *n.m.* − clothes, or most anything made from material (sheets, napkins, etc.)
Elle a mis tout son linge dans un sac vert. − She put all his clothes in a garbage bag.

Liqueur *n.f., Fr.* − after-dinner drink
- ✹ *liqueur douce* − soda, carbonated non-alcoholic drink

Liseux(euse) *n.m./fem., adj.* − bookworm, one who reads constantly

Lit *n.m., Fr.* − bed
- ✹ *grand lit double* − queen bed
- ✹ *lit double* − double bed
- ✹ *lit simple* − single bed
- ✹ *très grand lit double* − king bed

Loadé(e) *adj.* − 1. filled; 2. loaded with money
Le gars à qui appartient ce char-là, il est pas mal loadé. − The guy who owns that car is pretty loaded.

Loader *v.t.* − to load, to fill up

Logis *n.m., Fr.* − apartment, house, place of residence

Lotion après-rasage *n.m.* − after-shave lotion

Loup-marin *n.m.* − seal (*lit.* sea wolf)

Lousse *adj., n.m.* – 1. loose, slack, play; 2. generous (in a monetary sense)

> *Lui, il a toujours été un peu lousse avec son argent.* – He's always been pretty generous with his money.
>
> ✷ (se) lâcher lousse – to let oneself loose (to have fun, etc.)

Lumière *n.f.* – 1. *Fr.* light; 2. car's headlight; 3. traffic light

> *Attention, la lumière va changer!* – Watch it, the light's going to change!
>
> *Mets tes lumières!* – Put your lights on!

Lunch *n.m.* – lunch

> ✷ *boîte à lunch* – lunchbox

Luncher *v.i.* – to have lunch

Lyrer *v.i.* – to whimper

M

Ma *expr., def. "je vais"* – I'm going (to)

Mâchable *adj.* – chewable

Magané(e) *adj.* – 1. ruined, battered, wrecked; 2. exhausted
J'ai travaillé jusqu'à trois heures du matin, alors là je suis complètement magané. – I was at work 'til three in the morning, so now I'm completely wrecked.
Je pense que le fauteuil est un peu trop magané pour garder. – I think the couch is a bit too far gone to keep.

Maganer *v.t.* – 1. to damage, to cause harm to; 2. to treat something/someone badly
Je ne veux pas maganer mon veston. – I don't want to damage my suit jacket.

Magasinage *n.m.* – shopping

Magasiner *v.i.* – to go shopping

(se) Maigner de cul★★ to hurry up, to move one's ass

Main *n.f., Fr.* – hand; 2. main drag, main road in a town
On s'est promenés sur la main pendant trois heures. – We walked along the main drag for three hours.
❋ *avoir les mains pleines de pouces* – to be all thumbs

Maïs soufflé *n.m.* – popcorn

Mais que *conj.* – as soon as

Malin(e) *adj.* – 1. angry; 2. nasty, aggressive

Malle *n.f., def. Eng. "mail"* – mail
❋ *aller à malle* – to go get the mail

Maller *v.t.* – to mail, to send

Mal pris *expr.* – in trouble, in bad shape

Manche *n.f.* – handle
- ✱ *branler dans la manche* – to hesitate when making a decision (*lit.* to hesitate in the handle)

Manger *v.t.* – to eat
- ✱ *en manger une* – to "get it," to get in trouble, to be reprimanded (*lit.* to eat one)
- ✱ *Mange de la marde!*✱✱ – Eat shit!
- ✱ *Mange de la schnoute!*✱ – Eat shit!

manger ses bâs – 1. to be uncomfortable with one's speech or action (*sim.* open mouth, extract foot); 2. to worry or panic (*lit.* to eat one's socks)
- ✱ *Qu'est-ce que ça mange en hiver?* – What is (it) like? (*lit.* What does it eat in winter?)
- ✱ *se faire manger* – to get chewed out
- ✱ *se laisser manger la laine sur le dos* – to lose one's shirt, to be exploited (*lit.* to let the wool be eaten from your back)

Manquer: *v.* – 1. *Fr.* to miss; 2. to barely miss

J'ai manqué de frapper son char par deux pousses! – I missed hitting his car by two inches!
- ✱ *manquer le bateau* – to miss the boat (figuratively or literally)

Marche *n.f., Fr.* – a stroll, a walk
- ✱ *prendre une marche* – to take a walk

On va aller prendre une marche jusqu'à midi. – We're going to go for a walk until noon.

Marcher *v.i., Fr.* – 1. to work, to function properly; 2. to walk
- ✱ *marcher à mort* – to work beautifully (*lit.* to work to death)
- ✱ *marcher à planche* – to work perfectly (*lit.* to work flat-out)

Marde✱✱ *n.f., def.* "merde" – shit
- ✱ *mouche à marde*✱ – clinger, annoying individual whose presence can't be escaped (*lit.* shit-fly)

- *plein de marde*** – full of shit
- *tache à marde** – clinger, annoying individual whose presence can't be escaped (*lit.* shit-stain)

Mardeux(euse) *adj., n.m./f.* – lucky, fortunate (person)

se Marier *v.t.* – to marry

Maringouin *n.m.* mosquito

Marmaille *n.f.* – children, kids

en Masse *n.f.* – 1. a lot of, much of; 2. enough, plenty
Ça glisse en masse! – It's really slippery!
On en a en masse, merci. – We have plenty, thanks.

Matcher *v.t.* – 1. to put together, to match; 2. to be a match, to fit together
Je n'aurais dû jamais le croire, mais le tapis et les draps matchent vraiment bien ensemble. – I never would have believed it, but the rug and drapes really do go well together.

Matrone *n.f.* – 1. mother-in-law; 2. matron, head of a household

Mauditement bon *expr.* – wickedly good

Maususse* *expl.* – Moses

Mautadit *expl., def. "maudit"* – damn

Méchant(e) *adj., adv., Fr.* – 1. wicked, mean, nasty; 2. very, really
Ça va être méchant dur. – That's going to be really hard.
Lui, c'est un gars assez méchant. – He's a pretty mean guy.

Mèche *n.f., Fr.* – 1. fuse, wick; 2. hair highlights, coloured strands
Je vais ajouter des mèches bleues demain. – I'm going to add some blue highlights to my hair tomorrow.

- *avoir la mèche courte* – to have a short fuse, to be quick-tempered

Médaille *n.f.* – coin

- *deux côtés de la médaille* – both sides of the coin

(le) Meilleur des mondes *expr.* – an ideal world

Mêlant(e) *adj.* – confusing, disorienting
C'était mêlant un peu de voir les deux ensemble. – It was a bit confusing to see the two of them together.

Mêlé(e) *adj., Fr.* – confused, mixed up

de Même *adv.* – like this/that
Je n'aime pas les gars de même. – I don't like guys like that.

Même à ça *adv.* – even so

Mémérage *n.f.* – gossip, chit-chat

Mémère *n.m./fem., adj.* – talkative, loquacious (person)

Mémérer *v.i.* – to gossip, to chatter

Ménage *n.m., Fr.* – housework
✹ *chicane de ménage* – household argument

Méné *n.m.* – 1. minnow; 2. person with little weight or influence in a given situation
Même s'il est là depuis cinq ans, il est toujours un méné au bureau. – Although he's been there for five years, he still has no influence at the office.

Mener *v.t., Fr.* – to lead, to conduct
✹ *mener le diable* – to make a racket, cause a disturbance (*lit.* to lead the devil)

Menterie *n.f.* – lie, untruth

Mer *n.f., Fr.* – sea
✹ *C'est pas la mer à boire.* – It's easy (*lit.* It's not the sea to drink).

Messe *n.f., Fr.* – mass, usually Roman Catholic in a Québécois context.
✹ *avoir du monde à la messe* – to be crowded (*lit.* to have people at the mass)

Mets-en! *expr.* – That's for sure! Totally! (*lit.* Add some more!)

Mettre *v.t., Fr.* – to put/place

   ✻ *Mets ça dans ta pipe puis fume!* – Put that in your pipe and smoke it!

   ✻ *mettre les bars sur les T* – to cross your "T"s and dot your "I"s

   ✻ *mettre des gants blancs* – to handle with kid gloves, to treat gently

   ✻ *mettre la musique dans le tapis* – to play music at high volume (*lit.* to put music in the carpet)

   ✻ *se faire mettre*★★★ – to get laid, to have sex with someone
Il sortait ce soir juste pour essayer de se mettre. – He went out tonight just to try to get laid.

   ✻ *se mettre en crisse*★★ – to get pissed-off, to become angry

Miel *n.m., Fr.* – honey

   ✻ *mouche à miel* – honeybee

Mieux *adv., Fr.* – better

   ✻ *être mieux de* – to be better to
T'es mieux d'aller plus tôt. – It'd be better for you to go earlier.

Minou *n.f., Fr.* – 1. cat. 2. darling (term of endearment)

Minoucher *v.i.* – to caress, to kiss, to cuddle with (someone)

Minoucher *v.t.* – to flatter (someone), to butter (someone) up

Minoune *n.f.* – 1. old car; 2. cat, kitten; 3. affectionate word for a young girl
Oui, ma minoune? – Yes, my darling?

Misère *n.f.* – difficulty

   ✻ *avoir de la misère* – to have difficulty

Mitaine *n.f.* – mitten

   ✻ *faire à mitaine* – to do by hand (*lit.* to do by mitten)

Moffer *v.i.* – to mess up, to botch, to miss (something)
J'ai essayé lui faire du sushi, mais je l'ai complètement moffé. – I tried
to make him sushi, but I completely botched it.

Moine★★ *n.m.* – 1. *Fr.* monk; 2. dick, penis

Molle *n.f* – soft ice cream

Mollo *adv.* – chilled-out, relaxed

Monde *n.m., Fr.* – 1. world; 2. people
  ✶ *du ben bon monde* – friendly folk, good people
  ✶ *comme du monde* – as everyone else is (*lit.* as other folks)

faire Mononcle *adj.* – old-fashioned
Je ne veux pas amener le tapis avec moi, ça fait trop mononcle. – I
don't want to bring the carpet, it's too old-fashioned.
Ouais, ça fait un peu mononcle, mais ce n'est pas grave. – Yeah, it's a
bit old-style, but that's not a problem.

Montée *n.f.* – driveway

Monter *v., Fr.* – to go up, to rise
  ✶ *monter d'une coche* – to go up a notch, to improve

Mordée *n.f.* – bite
C'est sûr qu'il a pris une mordée dans ton profit. – It's certain that
he took a bite out of your profits.

Mort *n.f., Fr.* – death
  ✶ *à mort* – a lot, completely
  ✶ *son chien est mort* – to be done-in, to be finished (*lit.* his dog is
    dead)

Moto hors route *n.m.* – motocross

Motoneige *n.f., Fr.* – snowmobile

Motte (de neige) *n.f.* – snowball

Motton *n.m., Fr.* – bump, knot, lump
- ✹ *avoir le motton (dans le gorge)* – 1. to be choked up, to have a lump in one's throat; 2. to be wealthy
  Quand elle lui a dit qu'elle l'aimait, ça se voyait qu'il avait le motton. – When she told him she loved him, you could see how choked up he was.

Mouche *n.f., Fr.* – fly
- ✹ *mouche à cheval* – horsefly
- ✹ *mouche à chevreuil* – deerfly
- ✹ *mouche à feu* – lightning bug, firefly
- ✹ *mouche à marde*★ – clinger, annoying individual whose presence can't be escaped (*lit.* shit-fly)
- ✹ *mouche à miel* – honeybee
- ✹ *mouche à orignal* – horsefly (*lit* moosefly)

Moufette *n.m.* – skunk

Mouillasser *v.i.* – to drizzle, to sprinkle (light rain)

Mouillassseux(euse) *adj.* – rainy, drizzly

Mouiller *v.i., Fr.* – 1. to wet; 2. to be rainy, to be wet
Il va mouiller toute la fin de semaine. – It's going to rain the whole weekend.
- ✹ *mouillir à boire debout* – to be pouring rain (*lit.* to rain so you can drink standing up)

Moumoune *adj., n.m./fem.* – 1. wimp, wuss, fraidy-cat; 2. homosexual

Moumoute *n.f.* – hairpiece

Mourant(e) *adj.* – hysterical, hilarious
J'ai vu ce film-là. C'était mourant! – I saw that film. It was a riot!

Mouton *n.m., Fr.* – sheep
- ✹ *revenir à ses moutons* – to come back to the subject at hand (*lit.* to get back to one's sheep)

Mouve *n.m.* – move (both to change place and to change feelings)
C'est un mouve que je ne peux vraiment pas expliquer. – That's a
move I really can't explain.

Mouver *v.i.* – to move (change residences)

Moyens *n.m. pl., Fr.* – the means, the methods, the techniques
Avez-vous un moyen de le faire livrer chez moi? – Do you have a
way to get it delivered to my place?
Il n'a pas les moyens financiers pour déménager à Westmount. – He
doesn't have the financial means to move to Westmount.

MTS *n.f. pl., abbr.* "*maladie transmise sexuellement*" – STD (sexually
transmitted disease).

Musique à bouche *n.f.* – harmonica

N

Nanane *n.m.* – 1. candy; 2. treat, goodie

Elle pleure parce qu'elle n'a pas eu son nanane. – She's crying because she didn't get her goodie.

Narc *n.m.* – drug squad, narcotics law enforcement

Necker *v.i.* – to make out, to neck, to kiss

Neige *n.f., Fr.* – snow

- *la neige folle* – very fluffy snow, powder snow
- *motte de neige* – snowball

Neiger *v.i., Fr.* – to snow

- *avoir vu neiger* – to have experience (*lit.* to have seen it snow)

Neo-Québécois *n.m./f.* – person recently immigrated to Quebec, the opposite of a Québécois *pur laine.*

Ne pas valoir de la colle *expr.* – to be worthless, to be of bad quality (*lit.* to not be worth glue)

Nerf *n.m., Fr.* – nerve

- *tomber sur les nerfs* – to annoy, to exasperate (*lit.* to fall on one's nerves)
- *Les nerfs!* – Chill out! Calm down!

Net-fret-sec *expr.* – cut and dry (*lit.* clean-cold-dry)

Nettoyeur *n.m.* – dry cleaner

(au) Neutre *n.m.* – (in) neutral gear (in a car)

Nez *n.m., Fr.* – nose

- *avoir le nez brun* – to be a brown-noser
- *respirer par le nez* – to calm down (*lit.* to breathe through the nose)

Niaisage *n.m.* – fooling around, silliness, stupidity

Niaiser *v.i.* – 1. to tease, to annoy; 2. to string someone along, to waste someone's time

* *niaiser avec la puck* – to waste time (*lit.* stop fooling around with the puck)

Niaiseux(euse) *n.m./fem., adj.* – idiot(ic), fool(ish)
T'es ben niaiseux! – You're a real pain!

NIP *n.m.* – PIN code, password (for a bank machine)

Nœud *n.m., Fr.* – knot

* *frapper un nœud* – to hit a wall, to encounter a significant obstacle

Noirceur *n.f.* – blackness, darkness

Nombril du monde *expr.* – egocentric person (*lit.* belly button of the earth)

* *(se) prendre pour le nombril du monde* – to believe oneself to be the most important thing (*lit.* to take oneself as the belly button of the earth)

Nono(Nounoune) *adj., n.m./fem.* – idiot, bozo, imbecile
Sois pas nounoune, toi! – Don't be an idiot!

Noune★★★ *n.f.* – reference to female genitalia

Nounours *n.m.* – teddy bear

Nous-autres *pron.* – we all, we

Nouveau *n.m., Fr.* – something new

* *attendre du nouveau* – to be expecting a child, to be pregnant (*lit.* to wait for a new one)

Nu-bas *expr.* – in socks (*lit.* nude socks)

O

Objecter *v.i.* – to object, to oppose

Occasions *n.f. pl.* – bargains

Œuf *n.m., Fr.* – egg
- ❋ *œufs (au) miroir* – eggs over easy
- ❋ *œufs brouillés* – scrambled eggs

Oignon *n.f., Fr.* – onion
- ❋ *s'habiller en pelures d'oignons* – to dress in layers (*lit.* to dress in onion skins)

Onguent *n.m.* – medicinal cream
- ❋ *ne pas être de l'onguent* – to not be expensive (*lit.* to not be medicinal cream)
  Mets-en, c'est pas de l'onguent. – Go ahead, add more, it's not that expensive.

OPC *expr., contr.* "au plus crissant" – as quickly as possible

Opérer *v.t., Fr.* – 1. to operate; 2. to make
- ❋ *faire opérer* – to make something function/work

Ordi(n) *n.m., abbr.* "ordinateur" – computer

Ordinaire *adj.* – mediocre, of moderate quality

Oreille *n.f., Fr.* – ear
- ❋ *avoir les oreilles dans le crin* – 1. to be careful, fearing something or someone; 2. to be in a bad mood (*lit.* to have one's ears in horsehair)
- ❋ *oreille de crisse* – pork rinds, fried salted pig fat; a traditional Québécois dish served in a *cabane à sucre.*
- ❋ *se faire monter les oreilles* – to get a haircut (*lit.* to get one's ears lifted)

Orignal *n.m.* – moose
> ✸ *câler l'orignal* – to throw up, to puke (*lit.* to call the moose)

Orteil *n.m., Fr.* – toe
> ✸ *se lever le gros orteil au nord* – to get up on the wrong side of the bed, to be cranky (*lit.* to get up with one's big toe pointed north)

Ostic★ *expl., def.* *"ostie"* – darn, gosh darn

Ostie★★ *expl.* – goddam; derived from the French word for "host," from the Catholic liturgy.

Ostinage *n.m.* – argument, disagreement

Ostination *n.f.* – arguement, disagreement

s'Ostiner *v.* – to argue, to disagree
C'est sûr qu'il va m'ostiner là-dessus. – It's certain that he'll argue with me about it.

Ostineux(euse) *n.m./f., adj.* – argumentative (person)

Ou *prep., Fr.* – or, else
> ✸ *oubedon (contr. "ou bien donc")* – or else.

Ouache! *interj.* – Yuck!

Ouair *v.t., def.* *"voir"* – to see
On va ouair un bon show ce soir. – We'll see a good show tonight.

Ouaouaron *n.m.* – large frog

Oubedon *expr., def.* *"ou bien donc"* – otherwise, or else

Oublie ça *expr.* – forget it

Oui allô *expr.* – hello; used when answering the telephone

Ouin *n.m.* – yeah
> ✸ *Ouin, pis?* – Yeah, so?

Oupelaye! *interj.* – 1. Whoa!; 2. Oups!, Whoops!

Ours *n.m., Fr.* – bear
> ✻ *un ours mal-lêché* – a scruffy person (*lit.* a badly licked bear)

Ouvrage *n.m.* – work

Ousque *expr., def.* "*où est-ce que*" – where is
> ✻ *Ousquilé?* – Where is he?

P

Pagette *n.f.* – pager, beeper

Pagosse *n.f.* – thing, object

Pain *n.m., Fr.* – bread
* *être né pour un petit pain* – born to be mediocre (*lit.* to be born for little bread)

Palettes *n.f. pl.* – front teeth

Palmarès *n.m.* – hit list, top 40

Pancarte *n.f.* – sign

Panneau *n.m.* – sign

Pantalon court *n.f.* – shorts

Pantoute *expr., def.* "pas en toute" – not at all, not entirely
* *Pas pire, pantoute!* – Not bad, not bad at all!

Papier sablé *n.f.* – sandpaper

Paquet *n.m.* – a bunch of, a lot of
* *paquet d'affaires* – a bunch of things

Paqueté(e) *adj.* – 1. loaded, drunk; 2. completely filled, packed (*lit.* stuffed)
* *(se) paqueter la fraise* – to get drunk
* *(se) paqueter la gueule* – to get drunk

Paquéter *v.t.* – to pack (bags, etc.)
* *paquéter ses petits* – to get ready to leave (*lit.* to pack one's little [things])

se Paqueter *v.i.* – to get loaded, to get drunk

Paraître bien/mal *v.i.* – to appear well/badly off

Parcomètre *n.m.* – parking meter

Pardessus *n.m.* – 1. overcoat; 2. rubbers, boots

Pareil(le) *adj.* – 1. *Fr.* same; 2. even so
Sa mère lui avait dit non, mais elle a fait ça pareil. – Her mom told her no, but she did it anyway.
✱ *pareil comme* – the same as

Parenté *n.f.* – extended family (aunts, uncles, cousins, etc.)

Par exemple *adv., interj.* – 1. actually; 2. *Fr.* for example; 3. however, though
Je n'y suis pas allé, par exemple. – I didn't go, actually.
Moi, par exemple, je ne suis pas encore convaincu. – I, however, am not yet convinced.

pas Parlable *adj.* – incommunicative, unable to be spoken with/to
Il est fâché en ce moment et pas très parlable. – He's mad right now and not very communicative.

Parler *v.i., Fr.* – to talk, to speak
✱ *parler à travers son chapeau* – to blow hot air, to speak without actual knowledge (*lit.* to speak across one's hat)
✱ *parler dans le dos* – to talk behind someone's back
✱ *parler les baguettes en l'air* – to gesticulate while talking

Parlure *n.f.* – slang

Partie des sucres *n.f.* – party or meal traditionally held at a sugar shack (*cabane à sucre*) in the springtime.

Partir *v.i.* – 1. *Fr.* to leave; 2. to start

On va bientôt partir. – We're going to leave soon.
Veux-tu partir le micro-ondes, s'il te plaît? – Would you start the microwave, please?
✱ *partir en affaires* – to start a business
✱ *partir pour la gloire* – 1. to head off on a mission; 2. to be pregnant (*lit.* to head off to glory)

✻ *partir sur une go* – to go on a bender, to go all out

✻ *partir sur une gosse** – to leave (somewhere) quickly

Pas d'affaire! *expr* – There's no question !

Pas d'allure *n.m./f.* – gauche or maladroit person

Passage *n.m.* – corridor, hall

Passe-passe *n.m.* – workaround, alternative method

se Passer *v.i.* – 1. *Fr.* to pass, pass off; 2. to give, to loan
As-tu trois dollars à me passer? – Could you loan me three bucks?

✻ *passer au cash* – to get what one deserves

✻ *passer au dép(anneur)* – to swing by the convenience store

✻ *passer au feu* – to burn down

✻ *passer la nuit sur la corde à linge* – to sleep badly (*lit.* to sleep on the clothesline)

✻ *passer proche de (faire quelque chose)* – to come close to (doing something)

✻ *passer sur l'autre bord* – to die

✻ *passer sur l'autre coté* – to die

✻ *passer tout droit* – to oversleep (*lit.* to go right through)

✻ *se faire passer (quelque chose) en dessous du nez* – miss a good occasion (*lit.* to have [something] go right under your nose)

✻ *se faire passer un citron* – to be handed a lemon, to be handed a dud

✻ *se faire passer un sapin* – to be had, to get a bad deal (*lit.* to be handed a fir tree)

Pas-vite *adj., n.m./fem.* – slo-mo, slow (person)

Patate *n.f.* – potato

✻ *bibite à patates* – cockroach

✻ *être dans les patates* – to be in error, to be mistaken (*lit.* to be in the potatoes)

✻ *faire patate* – to fail

✴ *Lâche pas la patate!* – Don't give up! (*lit.* Don't let go of the potato!)
✴ *patate de sofa* – couch potato
✴ *patates frites* – french fries
✴ *patates pillées* – mashed potatoes
✴ *patates sucrées* – sweet potatoes

Patché(e)★★ *adj.* – on the rag, having one's (female monthly) period

Patcher *v.t.* – to patch (up), to fix
✴ *patcher un pneu* – to patch a tire

Pâte à dents *n.f.* – toothpaste

Pâté chinois *n.m.* – an oven-baked casserole of ground beef, corn, and mashed potatoes, similar to shepherd's pie.

Patente *n.f.* – thing, object
✴ *patente à gosse* – gadget, small object
✴ *toute la patente* – the whole bit

Patenter *v.* – to patch together, to whip up, to invent

Patienter *v.i., Fr.* – to wait, to hold on
On s'excuse de vous avoir fait patienter. – We apologize for the wait.

Patiner *v.i., Fr.* – 1. to skate; 2. to move
Il faut qu'il patine vite s'il veut réussir. – He'd better get a move on if he wants to succeed.
✴ *accrocher ses patins* – to end one's career, give up (*lit.* to hang up one's skates)

Patof *n.m.* – clown; originates from a character in a popular 1970s children's TV show.

Patois *n.m.* – dialect, regional language

Pause *n.f.* – break; typically used on the radio to convey a "station break" (i.e., commercials).

Paver *v.t.* – to pave

Payer *v., Fr.* – to pay
> ✸ *payer la traite (à quelqu'un)* – to pay (someone's) way

Peau *n.f., Fr.* – skin
> ✸ *peau de carriole* – carriage blanket; typically refers to a blanket found in horse-drawn carriages (*lit.* cart skin).

Pédaler *v.i.* – 1. to pedal or push with one's feet; 2. to make an effort
Il faut que tu pédales plus vite si tu veux réussir. – You need to make more of an effort if you want to succeed.
> ✸ *pédaler dans le beurre* – make useless efforts (*lit.* to pedal in butter)

Peignure *n.f.* – haircut

Peinturer *v.* – to paint

Pelleter des nuages *expr.* – to dream, usually of something unrealistic (*lit.* to shovel clouds)

Pelure *n.f., Fr.* – skin, outer layer
> ✸ *enlever une pelure* – to remove one's coat (*lit.* to take off a layer)
> ✸ *s'habiller en pelures d'oignons* – to dress in layers (*lit.* to dress in onion skins)

Pend-oreilles *n.m. pl.* – earrings

Penser *v.i., Fr.* – to think
> ✸ *penser croche* – to think dirty (sexual sense)

Pentré *n.m.* – kitchen or bathroom counter

Pépin *n.m* – inconvenience, problem

Peppé(e) *adj.* – psyched, enthusiastic, pepped up

Péquiste *n.m./f.* – supporter of the Parti Québécois

Perdre *v., Fr.* – to lose
- ✱ *perdre la track* – to go nuts, to lose one's head (*lit.* to lose the track)
- ✱ *perdre sa salive* – to waste one's breath (*lit.* to lose one's saliva)

Peser *v.t.* – to push, to depress
- ✱ *peser sur la suce* – to step on the gas
- ✱ *peser sur le gaz* – to step on the gas
- ✱ *peser sur (un bouton)* – to push on (a button)

Pétard *adj., n.m.* – knock-out, bombshell (attractive man or woman)

Péter★ *v.i., Fr.* – 1. to fail, to break down; 2. to pass wind, to fart; 3. to exhaust, to wear out
Ce programme-là va péter le reste du budget. – That program is going to blow the rest of the budget.
Son char va péter, c'est sûr. – His car is definitely going to break down.
- ✱ *péter au frette* – to drop dead (*lit.* to stop cold)
- ✱ *péter de la broue* – to brag about one's abilities (*lit.* to fart suds)
- ✱ *péter la balloune* – to fail a breathalyzer (alcohol) test
- ✱ *péter la balloune de (quelqu'un)* – to burst (someone's) bubble
- ✱ *péter la gueule en sang* – to knock someone's teeth out (*lit.* to explode the mouth with blood)
- ✱ *péter plus haut que le trou★* – 1. to live above one's means; 2. to be pretentious (*lit.* to pass wind above the hole)
- ✱ *péter une coche* – to blow a fuse, to become furious
- ✱ *se péter les bretelles* – to boast, to brag (*lit.* to snap one's suspenders)
- ✱ *Va donc péter dans les fleurs!* – Get outa here, will ya! (*lit.* Go fart in the flowers!)

Péteux(euse) de broue *expr.* – braggart

Petit change *n.m.* – loose change

Petit coin: *n.m* – potty, bathroom (*lit.* small corner)

Petit Crisse *n.m. /f.* – traitor, two-faced person
Méfie-toi, ce gars-là est un vrai petit crisse. – Better watch it, that guy is really two-faced.
(aux) Petites heures *expr.* – (to) the wee hours of the morning
Ils se sont laissés aux petites heures. – They parted ways in the wee hours of the morning.

Piasse *n.f., def. "piastre"* – buck, dollar..

Piastre *n.f.* – buck, dollar
As-tu trois piastres à me passer? – Do you have three bucks you could loan me?
> ✤ *avoir des yeux ronds comme des piastres* – to have eyes round like saucers
> ✤ *changer quatre trente sous pour une piastre* – 1. to make no profit; 2. to change one thing for another of identical value (*lit.* to change thirty cents for a quarter)
> ✤ *faire le piastre* – to make bucks, to make a lot of money

Pic *n.m., Fr.* – peak
> ✤ être à pic – to be grumpy, irritable

Pichou★★ *n.m.* – unattractive woman

Picosser *v.i.* – to rummage, to forage

Picrelle★★ *n.f.* – prostitute, tramp

Pied *n.m., Fr.* – 1. foot (body part); 2. foot (unit of measure)
> ✤ *avoir les deux pieds dans la même bottine* – to be clumsy, unresourceful (*lit.* to have both feet in the same boot)
> ✤ *être à pied* – to be in financial difficulty

Piger *v.t.* – to get, to grab, to take

Pigrasser *v.t.* – to screw around, to waste time

Pigrasseux(euse) *n.m. /f.* – one who wastes time

Pile *n.f.* – pile
> *Il laisse traîner des piles de ses affaires partout dans la maison.* – He leaves piles of his stuff all over the house.

Piler *v.* – 1. to peel, to scrape off; 2. to walk on, to walk over
> *Attention, tu viens de piler sur mes papiers!* – Watch it, you just walked on my papers!

Piment *n.m.* – pepper (vegetable)
> ✱ *piment fort* – hot pepper

Pinch *n.m.* – small beard encircling the mouth

Piner *v.i.* – to annoy, to bother, to harrass
> *Il me pine là-dessus depuis deux jours.* – He's been bothering me for two days about that.

Pinotte *n.f.* – peanut

Pinte *n.f.* – pint

Pipe *n.m.* – 1. *Fr.* (smoking) pipe; 2. lie, false story
> *Raconte-moi pas de pipes, je sais très bien ce qui est arrivé.* – Don't lie to me, I know very well what happened.

Piquer *v.t.* – to grab, to snatch
> ✱ *piquer une crise* – to throw a fit
> ✱ *piquer une jasette* – to have a chat

Piquetage *n.m.* – picketing

Piqueter *v.i.* – to picket (a place)

Pire *adj., Fr.* – worst, the worst, bad
> ✱ *au pire aller* – in the worst case
> ✱ *C'est pas pire!* – Not bad!
> ✱ *(de) pire en pire* – worse and worse
> ✱ *pas si pire* – not so bad
> ✱ *pas pire pantoute* – not bad, not bad at all

Pis *conj., def. "puis"* – 1. and, next; 2. so
> ✱ *Et pis?* – And so?
> ✱ *Pis toi?* – And you?

Pisse-minute *n.f.* – someone with a frequent need to visit the bathroom

Pissou *n.m.* – fraidy-cat, coward

Pitcher *v.t.* – to throw, to pitch
> *Je vais pitcher ça à la poubelle.* – I'm going to throw that out.

Piton *n.m.* – button (*impl.* any surface able to be pressed down)
> ✱ *être de bonne heure sur le piton* – to be up at the crack of dawn (*lit.* to be on the button early)
> ✱ *mettre la musique dans le piton* – to play music at high volume (*lit.* to put music in the button)
> ✱ *(ne pas être) sur le piton* – to (not be) ready

Pitonner *v.i.* – 1. to press a button; 2. to channel surf
> *Arrête de pitonner, toi!* – Stop changing channels!

Pitonneuse *n.f.* – remote control (for a TV, etc.)

Pitou *n.m.* – 1. pooch, dog; 2. child, kid (affectionate)
> *pauvre p'tit pitou* – poor little guy

Pitoune★★ *n.f.* – 1. over-dressed, over-made woman; 2. floating log (when transporting logs via a river, as done in the lumber industry); 3. token, bingo chip

Placer *v.* – to put, to place
> ✱ *placer un appel* – to place a call

Placotage *n.m.* – gossip, chatter

Placoter *v.i.* – to gossip, to chatter
> ✱ *placoter sur le dos de quelqu'un* – to talk behind (someone's) back
> *Ils n'arrêtaient pas de placoter sur le dos de Yannick.* – They gossiped non-stop about Yannick.

Plaisant(e) *adj.* – nice, pleasant

Plaisir *n.m., Fr.* – fun, pleasure
    ✱ *plaisir coupable* – guilty pleasure

Planche *n.f., Fr.* – board, plank
    ✱ *à planche* – all the way, completely
    On va faire ça à planche. – We'll do it all the way.
    ✱ *faire de la planche à neige* – to snowboard

Planification *n.f.* – planning

Planifier *v., Fr.* – to plan, to schedule

(se) Planter *v.i.* – to fail
    Ça va planter, sûr. – It's going to fail, for certain.
    Il va se planter au moment d'essayer. – He's going to fail as soon as he tries.

Plaster *n.m.* – adhesive bandage

Platée *n.f.* – plateful (of food)
    Ça, c'est toute une platée! – That's quite a plateful!

Platte *adj.* – 1. boring, annoying; 2. unfortunate
    C'est platte, ça! – That's a shame!
    Je la trouvais pas mal platte, son histoire. – I found his story pretty boring.
    ✱ *joke platte* – stupid joke

Plein *adj., Fr.* – full
    ✱ *(en) avoir plein son casque* – to have enough (*lit.* to have one's hat full)

Pleumer *v.t.* – to pluck (feathers, etc.)
    ✱ *se faire pleumer* – to get taken, to be had (*lit.* to get plucked)

Pleurnichard(e) *adj.* – a crybaby, easily crying

Pleuvoir *v.i., Fr.* – to rain

    ✱ *Il pleut à boire debout.* – It's raining very hard (*lit.* it's raining to drink standing up).

    ✱ *Il pleut des cordes* – It's raining very hard (*lit.* it's raining cords of wood).

Pli *n.m.* – fold, pleat

    ✱ *faire un pli* – to be bothered or upset by something; generally used in the negative.

    Ça ne me fait pas un pli. – That doesn't bother me at all.

Ploguer *v.t.* – to plug in, to connect

    Je vais l'ploguer dans le mur. – I'll plug it in the wall.

    Il est pas mal plogué dans l'industrie. – He's pretty well connected in the industry.

Plotte★★★ *n.f.* – 1. slut, whore; 2. female genitalia

    ✱ *avoir la plotte à terre*★★★ – to be exhausted

    ✱ *plotte à bike*★★★ – motorcycle girl

Pluie verglaçante *n.f.* – freezing rain

Plus ou moins *expr.* – more or less (generally implies less)

Poche *adj.* – bad, ugly

    Son dessin était pas mal poche. – His drawing was pretty bad.

Poche *n.f.* – male sexual organs

Pocher *v.t.* – to screw up, to do a bad job (on something)

Poêle *n.m.* – stove.

Poêlon *n.m.* – large stove

Pogné(e) *adj.* – stuck

    Je suis vraiment pogné là-dessus. – I'm really stuck on that point.

    ✱ *pogné dans une combine* – caught in a bad situation

Pogner *v.* − 1. to get, to receive; 2. to grab, to trap, to catch; 3. to have (sense of possession); 4. to quarrel, to argue; 5. to be successful (especially with the opposite sex)

> *C'est fou comment qu'il pogne, ce gars-là.* − It's amazing how well that guy does with women.
>
> *J'ai pogné un rhume.* − I caught a cold.
>
> *On a été pogné dans la neige pendant deux heures.* − We were stuck in the snow for two hours.

> ❋ *pogner le jackpot* − to hit the jackpot
> ❋ *pogner le Klondike* − to strike it rich, to succeed
> ❋ *pogner les nerfs* − to become irritable, angry
> ❋ *pogner son air* − to be surprised (*lit.* to take one's breath)
> ❋ *pogner une chicane* − to argue, to have a dispute
> ❋ *se faire pogner* − to get caught
> ❋ *se pogner le bacon* − to goof off, to do nothing
> ❋ *se pogner le cul* − to goof off, to do nothing.
> ❋ *se pogner le derrière* − to goof off, to do nothing

se Pogner *v.i.* − to hook up, to get together (romantically)

Poignée *n.f., Fr.* − handle

> ❋ *avoir une poignée dans le dos* − to be gullible (*lit.* to have a handle on one's back)

Poil *n.f., Fr.* − hair

> ❋ *Bibite à poil* − small animal
> ❋ *s'énerver le poil des jambes* − to get upset (*lit.* to irritate one's leg hair)
> ❋ *s'exciter le poil des jambes* − to get upset (*lit.* to excite one's leg hair)

Pointe *n.f.* − slice (of pizza or pie)

Pointer *v.t.* − to point out, to highlight

> *Il m'a pointé trois problèmes différents avec la compagnie.* − He pointed out three different problems with the company.

Poli à ongles *n.m.* − nail polish

Police montée *n.f.* – mounted police

Pommes de route *n.f. pl.* – horse droppings

Pompette *adj.* – drunk, intoxicated

Popoter *v.i.* – to cook, to prepare a meal

Poqué(e) *adj.* – 1. tired or hurt (for a person); 2. damaged (for an object); 3. trashed, very drunk (for a person)

Poquer *v.t.* – to damage, to dent, to ding

Porc *n.m., Fr.* – 1. pig; 2. pork
  ✱ *faire des yeux de porc frais* – to be wide-eyed (*lit.* to have eyes like a fresh pig)

Porter *v.t.* – to carry, to bring
  Je vais te porter une pizza ce soir. – I'll bring you a pizza tonight.

Possiblement *adv.* – possibly

Poste de TV *n.f.* – TV station

Poteau *n.m.* – post, telephone pole
  ✱ *sirop de poteau* – imitation maple syrup (*lit.* telephone pole syrup)

Potter *v.t.* – to sink (something)
  ✱ *potter un but* – to make a goal, to sink a puck (hockey)

Poucer *v.i.* – to hitchhike, to thumb a ride

Poudrerie *n.f.* – wind-blown snow

Poupoune *n.f.* – over-made, badly dressed woman

Pour *prép.* – 1. *Fr.* for; 2. according to, as for
  Pour moi, j'en ai marre. – As for me, I've had enough.
  ✱ *être pour (quelque chose)* – to be in favour of (something), to be all for (something)

Pourquoi (que) *adv., pron.* – why (the reason that); often used directly as a pronoun.

> *C'est pourquoi que je suis venu.* – That's why I came.

Pourriel *n.m.* – spam email

Pourtant *adv.* – nevertheless, yet

Pousse-pousse *n.m.* – stoller, carriage

Pousser *v.t., Fr.* – to push
> ✶ *être top poussé* – too far out, to far ahead
> *Ses idées sont bonnes, mais je trouve qu'elles sont un peu trop poussées pour notre organisation.* – His ideas are good, but I find them a bit too far ahead for our organization.

se Pousser *v.i.* – to head out, to take off

Pousseux(euse) *n.m. /f.* – hitchhiker

Poutine *n.f.* – 1. a mixture of french fries and cheese curds covered in gravy; 2. anything that is a mixture of various elements.
> *C'est toute la même poutine.* – It's all the same stuff.

(se) Pouvoir *v.i.* – to be possible, to be thinkable
> *Ça ne se peut pas qu'il y soit allé!* – There's no way he could've gone!
> ✶ *ça s'peut-tu que* – could it be that

(se) Practiquer *v.i.* – to practice

Prélart *n.m.* – linoleum
> ✶ *mettre la musique dans le prélart* – to play music at high volume (*lit.* to put music in the linoleum)

Prendre *v., Fr.* – to take.
> ✶ *ça prend* – that'll take; similar to *il faut*, is generally used to specify something necessary to identify a goal; also used in the reflexive (e.g., *ça me prend*).
> *Ça prend deux minutes de ton temps.* – It'll take two minutes of your time.

Ça va te prendre une cuillère pour le manger. – You'll need a spoon to eat it.

- *prendre ça aisé* – to take it easy
- *prendre la part de (quelqu'un)* – to take (someone's) side
- *prendre la passe du cochon qui tousse* – to cut corners, to take a shortcut (*lit.* to take the way of the coughing pig)
- *prendre le champs* – to drive off the road (*lit.* to take to the fields)
- *prendre offense* – to take offence
- *prendre (quelque chose) en note* – to make note of (something)
- *prendre son temps* – to take one's time
- *prendre tout son petit change* – to take all one's resources, to take great effort (*lit.* to take all one's spare change)
- *prendre un break* – 1. to take a break; 2. to stop dating someone temporarily (romantic sense)
- *prendre une brosse* – go on a bender, to get drunk
- *prendre une bouchée* – to grab a bite
- *prendre une chance* – to take a chance
- *prendre un coup* – to go drinking
- *prendre un cours* – to take a class
- *prendre une débarque* – to take a fall
- *prendre une fouille* – to take a fall
- *prendre une marche* – to go for a walk
- *prendre une touche* – to take a drag (on a cigarette, etc.)
- *se prendre pour le nombril du monde* – to believe oneself to be the most important thing (*lit.* to take oneself as the belly button of the earth)

Prérequis(e) *n.m., adj., Fr.* – requirement, prerequisite

Présentement *adv., Fr.* – currently, right now, presently

Press *n.f.* – urgency, haste

Pressage *n.m.* – ironing, pressing

Presser *v.t.* – to iron, to press

Prix de liste *n.m.* – list price

Problématique *n.f.* – a problematic situation
  ✹ *vider la problématique* – to get to the bottom of the problem

Proche *adj., Fr.* – near
  ✹ *passer proche de (faire quelque chose)* – to come close to (doing something)

(se) Promener *v.i., Fr.* – to walk, to wander
  ✹ *se promener en bedaine* – to go shirtless

Prometteux(euse) *adj.* – promising, hopeful
  Son projet n'avait pas l'air trop prometteux. – His project didn't seem terribly promising.

Puck *n.f.* – (hockey) puck
  ✹ *niaiser avec la puck* – to waste time (*lit.* to fool around with the puck)

Prudemment *adv.* – prudently, with caution

Pudding chômeur *n.m.* – simple, inexpensive pudding made from flour and brown sugar (*lit.* unemployed man's pudding)

Puffeux *n.m.* – windbag (for a person)

Pure laine *expr.* – dyed in the wool; often used to refer to a francophone Quebecer who can trace most (if not all) of their ancestry to the colony of New France (*lit.* pure wool).
  Lui, c'est un Québécois pure laine. – He's a dyed-in-the-wool Québécois.

Q

Quand que *conj.* – when, whenever

Quasiment *adv.* – almost, pretty much

Quatre-par-quatre *n.m.* – four-by-four, light truck

Queneuilles *n.f. pl.* – eyes

Quequ' *pron., def.* "*quelque chose*" – and some; used after numbers to imply an approximate amount.
> *Ça m'a coûté trois cents quequ' pour réparer mon char.* – It cost me three hundred and something to fix my car.
> *Cent quequ'* – one hundred and some

Quequ' chose *pron., contr.* "*quelque chose*" – something

Quéquette★ *n.f.* – dick, penis
> ★ *Grosse corvette, petite quéquette!* –. a saying used for a wealthy but immature person (*lit.* Large corvette, small dick!).

Quequ' part *adv., contr.* "*quelque part*" – somewhere

Quessé? *expr., def.* "*qu'est-ce que c'est?*" – What is it?

Questa? *expr., def.* "*Qu'est-ce que tu as?*" – What do you have? What's wrong?

Quétaine *adj.* – tasteless, bad
> ★ *quétaine au boutte* – completely tasteless
> *Ces vêtements sont quétaines au boutte.* – These clothes are completely tasteless.

Quétainerie *n.f.* – crap, object in bad taste
> *Sa maison est superbe, mais la quétainerie qu'il a sur les murs la défait complètement.* – His house is amazing, but the crap he has on the walls totally wrecks it.

Quêter *v.i.* – to beg

Quêteux(euse) *n.m./fem., adj.* – beggar

Quille *n.f.* – bowling pin
  ✱ *jouer aux quilles* – to bowl, to go bowling

Quitter *v.i.* – to leave, to head out

Quoi *pron., Fr.* – what
  ✱ *de quoi* – something, anything
  As-tu de quoi à faire? – Do you have anything to do?

R

Rabais *n.m.* – rebate, discount

Raboudinage *n.m.* – botched-up work

Raboudiner *v.t.* – to botch, to mess up

Rackadjo *n.m., contr.* "rack à jos" – breasts

(se) Racoquiller *v.i.* – to cower

Ragoût de pattes *n.m.* – traditional Québécois fare made from pig's feet and beef meatballs in a rich brown stew.

Raide *adj.* – stiff
* ❋ *ben raide* – completely, totally (*lit.* good and stiff)
* ❋ *fou raide* – completely nuts
* ❋ *fucké ben raide*★★ – completely screwed up
* ❋ *raide comme une barre* – stiff as a bar

(se) Ramasser *v.t.* – to wind up (somewhere), end up (somewhere)
Après un bout, on s'est ramassés ici. – After a bit, we ended up here.
* ❋ *se faire ramasser* – to be called on the carpet (for something), to get in trouble

Rang *n.m.* – 1. *Fr.* rank (in an organization); 2. country road
* ❋ *école de rang* – country(side) school

(se) Raplomber *v.i.* – to find one's balance

Raqué(e) *adj.* – tired, exhausted, destroyed
Je suis trop raqué pour sortir à soir. – I'm too exhausted to go out tonight.

Raquettes *n.f. pl.* – (humerous) term for someone's (oversized) feet

Ras (au) *adj.* – near, close (to)

Rase-trou *n.m.* – short item of female clothing (such as a skirt) that is at the limit of good taste (*lit.* scrape-hole)

Ratoureux(euse) *n.m./fem., adj.* − wily, sly, crafty

Rattrapable *adj.* − able to be caught

Ravage *n.m.* − trail

Rayé(e) *adj.* − scratched, scraped, dinged

Rayer *v.* − to scratch, to scrape

Razbol *n.m.* − bowl cut (haircut)

Recevoir *v., Fr.* − to receive
> ✖ *recevoir quelque chose sur la tomate* − be hit by something unexpected (*lit.* to catch something on the tomato)

Réchauffé(e) *adj.* − 1. *Fr.* reheated 2. loaded, drunk

Recherchiste *n.m./f.* − researcher

Référer *v.* − to refer, to pass on

Regarder *v., Fr.* − to look
> ✖ *regarder bien pour* − to look good for
> *Ça regarde bien pour demain!* − Everything looks good for tomorrow!

Réguine *n.f.* − device or item that doesn't work as expected, a lemon
> *La tondeuse que j'ai achetée est une vraie réguine, ça fonctionne une fois sur deux.* − The lawnmower I bought is a real lemon, it works one time out of two.

Régulier(ière) *adj.* − normal, standard

Rejet *n.m.* − loser, reject
> *Ce gars-là est un rejet.* − That guy is a loser.

Rejoindre *v.t.* − 1. *Fr.* to meet, to come together; 2. to contact, to get a hold of, to catch (up with) someone
> *Tu peux le rejoindre chez lui.* − You can catch him at home.

Remorqueuse *n.f.* − tow-truck

Remplissage *n.m.* – refill
   ✱ *remplissage gratuit* – free refill

Renforcir *v.t.* – to strengthen

Renipper *v.t.* – to fix up, to repair
   Mon chum a renippé son char l'été dernier. – My boyfriend fixed up his car last summer.

Rentrer *v.i., Fr.* – to re-enter (a house or other structure), to go home
   ✱ *(se) faire rentrer dedans* – 1. to be hit (by a vehicle or object); 2. to be scolded or otherwise verbally berated

Renvoyer *v.t.* – 1. to send back, to send away; 2. to vomit, to throw up
   J'ai renvoyé le colis le lendemain. – I sent the package back the next day.
   ✱ *se faire renvoyer* – 1. to be sent away; 2. to lose one's job

Réseautage *n.m.* – networking, social interaction

Résident(e) *n.m./fem., Fr.* – resident, inhabitant

Resoudre *v.i.* – to arrive uninvited

Respirer *v.i., Fr.* – to breathe
   ✱ *respirer par le nez* – to calm down (*lit.* to breathe through the nose)

Ressorer *v.* – to spin

Restable *adj.* – livable, decent (*lit.* stay-able)
   On a quitté assez vite puisque le bar n'était pas très restable. – We left pretty quickly since the bar wasn't very decent.

Rester *v.i.* – 1. *Fr.* to stay; 2. to live, to habitate in
   On reste à Jonquière en ce moment. – We're living in Jonquière at the moment.
   ✱ *rester assis sur son steak* – to sit on one's butt, to not do anything

Restituer *v.* – to vomit

Retontir *v.i.* – to arrive uninvited
Georges a tendance à retontir à l'heure du souper. – George tends to arrive uninvited around dinnertime.

Retourner *v., Fr.* – to return, to revisit
✱ *retourner un appel (téléphonique)* – to call back, to return someone's (telephone) call

Retracer *v.t.* – to find again, to rediscover
On n'a jamais pu retracer le même chemin pour retourner. – We were never able to find the way back there.

Revenir *v.i., Fr.* – to return, to come back
✱ *revenir à (ses) moutons* – to come back to the subject at hand (*lit.* to get back to [one's] sheep)

Revirer *v.i.* – to swing around, to turn around, to reverse course
Je vais revirer vers Montréal. – I'm going to turn back toward Montreal.
✱ *(se) revirer sur un trente sou* – to turn on a dime

Revoler *v.t.* – to fly apart, to scatter

Ricaneux(euse) *n.m./fem., adj.* – mocking, scoffing

Rider *v.t.* – to push (someone) hard, to ride someone

Rien *pron., Fr.* – nothing
✱ *Il n'y a rien là.* – It's nothing.

Rince-bouche *n.m.* – mouthwash

Rincer *v.t., Fr.* – to rinse
✱ *se rincer le bec* – to have a drink (*lit.* to rinse one's beak)

Rire *v.i., Fr.* – to laugh
✱ *rire comme un défonçé* – to die laughing

Robine *n.f.* – rotgut, bad-quality alcohol

Robineux(euse) *n.m./fem.* – drunkard, bum

Rond(e) *adj., Fr.* – round
* ✴ *être rond comme une bine* – to be completely sloshed/drunk (*lit.* to be as round as a bean)

Rondelette *adj.f.* – chubby, overweight (used for a girl or woman)

Rondouillette *n.f.* – chubby, overweight woman

Roteux *n.m.* – hot dog

Rôties *n.m. pl.* – toast

Rouge *n.m., Fr.* – red
* ✴ *être dans le rouge* – to be in the red, to be in financial difficulty
* ✴ *voir rouge* – to see red, to be angry

Rouler *v.t., Fr.* – to roll
* ✴ *rouler sa bosse* – to show one's wisdom (*lit.* to roll one's bump)

Rouleuse *n.f.* – hand-rolled cigarette

Roulotte *n.f.* – trailer, camper
* ✴ *roulotte à patates* – mobile food stand selling french fries

Route pavée *n.f.* – paved road

Roux(sse) *adj.* – russet, brownish-red; a popular women's hair colour

Ruban (adhésif) *n.m.* – (adhesive) tape

Rubber *n.m.* – 1. tire; 2. boots; 3. condom

Ruine-babines *n.f.* – harmonica

Runnings: *n.m. pl.* – running shoes

Rushant(e) *adj.* – hurried, rushing, stressful
Mon travail était rushant. – My job was stressful.

Rusher *v.i.* – to be in a rush

S

Sa *expr., contr.* "sur la" – on the

Sabler *v.t.* – to sand (using sandpaper)

Sacoche *n.f.* – handbag, pocketbook
> ✻ *sacoche d'école* – school bag

Sacrament! *interj.* – By all that's holy!

Sacrant(e) *adj.* – annoying, aggravating
> ✻ *au plus sacrant* – as quickly as possible

Sacre *n.m.* – oath, blasphemy

Sacrer *v.i.* – 1. to swear, to curse; 2. to put or place something in a careless manner; 3. not to care
> *J'ai sacré ta jupe sur le comptoir.* – I threw your dress on the counter.
> *Je m'en sacre si tu veux pas y aller!* – I don't give a damn if you don't want to go!
> *Il a descendu tous les saints du ciel tant y a sacré.* – He swore so much that he brought all the saints down from the heavens.
> ✻ *sacrer la paix* – to leave (someone) alone
> *Pourrais-tu me sacrer la paix, s'il te plaît?* – Could you give me a little peace, please?
> ✻ *sacrer (quelqu'un) dehors* – to throw (someone) out
> ✻ *sacrer son camp★* – to leave, to head out
> ✻ *se faire sacrer à la porte* – to be thrown out (of a job)

Salle de montre *n.f* – showroom

Sans-dessein(ne) *adj., n.m./fem.* – clueless, thoughtless (person)

Saper *v.i.* – to chew with one's mouth open

Sapin *n.m., Fr.* – fir tree
> ✻ *(se faire) passer un sapin* – to be had, to get a bad deal (*lit.* to be handed a fir tree)

Sarrau *n.m.* – medical jacket

(se) Saucer *v.t.* – to dip onseself (gradually) in water, to get wet

Saucette *n.f.* – 1. brief visit; 2. a dip in a pool, etc.
* ✷ *faire une saucette* – to go for a dip
  On va faire une saucette dans la piscine. – We're going to take a dip in the pool.

Saut *n.m.* – jump, start
* ✷ *faire un saut* – to jump, to start
  J'ai fait un saut quand il a ouvert la porte. – I jumped when he opened the door.

Sauté(e) *adj.* – 1. incredible, unbelievable, mind-blowing; 2. crazy, insane (for a person) (*lit.* jumped)
  J'ai vu ce film hier. C'est complètement sauté! – I saw that film yesterday. It was just mind-blowing.

Sauter *v.t., Fr.* – to jump, to leap
* ✷ *sauter la clôture* – to cheat on one's spouse (*lit.* to jump the gate)
* ✷ *sauter une coche* – to blow a fuse, to become furious
* ✷ *sauter un gasket* – to blow a gasket, to become furious

Sauver *v.t.* – to save, to conserve

se Sauver *v.i., Fr.* – to escape, to leave in a hurry
  Il va se sauver de la partie bientôt. – He's going to leave the party soon.

Scalper *v.t.* – to scalp tickets

Schnoute★ *n.f.* – shit
* ✷ *Mange de la schnoute!* – Eat shit!

Scie à chaîne *n.f.* – chainsaw

Scorer *v.t.* – 1. to score a goal; 2. to score in the sexual sense

Scrammer *v.i.* – to scram, to leave quickly

Scrappe *n.f.* – junk
    Mon char, c'est de la scrappe. – My car is a heap.
    ✸ *cour à scrap* – junkyard

Scrapper *v.t.* – 1. to throw out, to trash (something); 2. to crash (while skiing, etc.)
    J'ai scrappé mon vélo l'autre jour. – I trashed my bike the other day.

Scratcher *v.t.* – to scratch (something)

S'cuze! *expr., def.* *"Excuse-moi!"* – Excuse me!
    ✸ *s'cuzez là* – thank you very much; often heard at the end of traditional Québécois songs.

Sécheuse *n.f.* – drying machine, dryer

Séchoir *n.m.* – hair dryer

Secousse *n.f.* – a while, a period of time
    Ça fait une secousse que je n'y suis pas allé. – It's been a while since I've been there.

Seineux(euse) *n.m./fem.* – busybody

Sent-bon *n.m.* – perfume, eau de toilette

Senteux(euse) *adj., n.m./fem.* – curious, nosy, tactless (person)

Sentir *v.i., Fr.* – 1. to feel; 2. to smell
    ✸ *sentir le swing* – to smell of sweat
    ✸ *sentir l'yâble* – to smell awful (*lit.* to smell the devil)
    ✸ *se sentir (tout) croche* – to feel (really) bad, to be unhappy

Séparatiste *n.m./fem., adj.* – one who supports the political separation of Quebec from Canada.

Séraphin *n.m.* – miser

Serre-la-piastre *n.m./f.* – miser, greedy person (*lit.* coin-hugger)

Serrer *v.t.* – 1. *Fr.* to squeeze, to tighten; 2. to put away
  Veux-tu me serrer ça? – Would you please put that away for me?
  ✱ *(se) serrer la babiche* – to tighten one's belt, to cut down

Serviable *adj.* – usable, workable

Set carré *n.m.* – square dance

Shafter *v.* – to give (someone) the shaft, to screw over

Shaker *v.i.* – to tremble, to shake (from fright, etc.)

Sharp *adj.* – 1. smart (for a person); 2. nice, appealing, cool, great

Shiner *v.t.* – to shine
  ✱ *shiner (ses) souliers* – to shine (one's) shoes

Shipper *v.t.* – to send, to ship
  Je vais lui shipper la boîte demain. – I'll ship him the box
  tomorrow.

Shirer *v.i.* – 1. to shear, to twist sideways; 2. to slide
  Mon char a shiré sur la glace. – My car slid on the ice.

Shooter *v.* – 1. to send, transmit. 2. to shoot
  Shoote-moi le fichier et je l'imprimerai. – Shoot me over the file,
  and I'll print it out for you.

Siffleux *n.m.* – marmot

Signaler *v.t.* – 1. to indicate (especially by depressing a button on a
phone); 2. to signal
  Pour rejoindre le téléphoniste, signalez le 0. – To reach the operator,
  press 0.

Simonaque *expr.* – dammit

Sirop de poteau *n.m.* – imitation maple syrup (*lit.* telephone pole
syrup)

Sirop d'érable *n.m.* – maple syrup

Slaquer *v.i.* – to goof off, to relax

Sloune *n.f.* – (beach) sandal, flip-flop

Smatte *adj.* – 1. pleasant, nice; 2. show-off
- ✖ *beau smatte* – one who disappoints by his/her behaviour
- ✖ *faire son smatte* – to show off

Soda à pâte *n.f* – baking soda (bicarbonate of soda)

Soignable *adj.* – able to be healed

Soir *n.m., Fr.* – evening
- ✖ *drette à soir* – as of this evening

Son chien est mort *expr.* – to be done-in, to be finished (*lit.* his dog is dead)

Songé(e) *adj.* – wise, insightful, thought-through
Il n'est pas le gars le plus songé du monde. – He's not the most brilliant guy in the world.

Sortir *v.i., Fr.* – to leave, to depart
Je ne peux pas m'en sortir encore. – I can't get out of it yet.
- ✖ *sortir du bois* – to make it out of the woods, to escape trouble
- ✖ *sortir du garde-robe* – to come out of the closet, to reveal one's homosexuality

Sou *n.m.* – cent, penny
Est-ce que t'as un vingt-cinq sous? – Do you have a quarter?
- ✖ *(se) revirer sur un trente sou* – to turn on a dime (*lit.* to turn on a quarter)

Soubassement *n.m.* – (sub)basement

Soue *n.f.* – sty
- ✖ *Ferme ta soue!* – Shut your trap! (*lit.* Shut your sty!)
- ✖ *soue à cochons* – pigsty

Souffler *v.t.* – to inflate, to blow up

Je vais souffler les ballons pour les enfants. – I'm going to blow up the balloons for the kids.

✻ *souffler dans la balloune* – to take a breathalyzer test (*lit.* to blow in the balloon)

Souffleuse *n.f.* – 1. snowblower; 2 snowplow

Soule *adj., Fr.* – drunk

✻ *soule comme une botte* – completely wasted, inebriated (*lit.* as drunk as a boot)

Souliers *n.m. pl.* – (low-cut) shoes

Soûlon(ne) *adj., n.m./fem.* – drunk, intoxicated

Soupane *n.f.* – oatmeal

Soupe *n.f., Fr.* – soup

✻ *voir (quelqu'un) dans ma soupe* – to be caught up with someone, to be head over heels for someone (*lit.* to see [someone] in my soup)

Souper *n.m.* – dinner, evening meal

✻ *souper communautaire* – pot-luck dinner

Sous *adv., Fr.* – below, under.

Il fait quarante degrés sous zéro. – It's forty degrees below zero.

✻ *sous l'impression (que)* – under the impression (that)

Sous-contracteur *n.m.* – subcontractor

Sous-marin *n.m.* – submarine (sandwich)

Sous-plat *n.m.* – hot plate

Souverainiste *n.m./fem., adj.* – one who supports the political separation of Quebec from Canada.

Spinner *v.t.* – to spin (around)

Splitter *v.t.* – to split, to divide
Pour la facture, veux-tu la splitter? – As for the check, shall we split it?

Spotter *v.t.* – to notice, to spot
On s'est fait spotter tout de suite. – We were noticed right away.

Squeegee *n.m./fem.* – an adolescent who cleans windshields at traffic lights to earn money.

Squeezer *v.* – to squeeze, to fit

Stacose (que) *expr., def. "c'est à cause (que)"* – because, since

Staller *v.* – to stall, to deliberately delay
Son projet a pas mal stallé. – His project has pretty much stalled.

Stationnement *n.m.* – parking lot

Stationner *v.* – to park (a car)

Steak *n.m., Fr.* – steak, beef
✱ *être assis sur son steak* – 1. to sit on one's butt, to be lazy; 2. to be in a comfortable financial position (*lit.* to be seated on one's steak)

Stepper *v.i.* – to start or jump (from surprise)
Quand il m'a parlé, ça m'a tellement surpris que j'ai steppé. – When he spoke to me, it surprised me so much that I started.

Stock *n.m.* – stuff; *c.f.* Stuff

Stoné(e) *adj.* – stoned (on drugs)

Straight *adj.* – conservative, law-abiding, up-front

S'tu *expr., def. "est-ce que c'est"* – is it that

Stuff *n.m.* – stuff; unlike in English, used only to refer to a single object of uncountable quality, such as a medicinal cream, a volume of liquid or powder, etc.

As-tu ajouté le stuff que t'as amené au punch? – Did you add that stuff you brought to the punch?

T'es-tu coupé? J'ai du stuff à mettre dessus, si tu veux. – Did you cut yourself? I have some stuff to put on that, if you want.

Suce *n.f.* – 1. sucker (for an infant); 2. car's accelerator
  ✱ *peser sur la suce* – to step on the gas

Suce-la-cenne *n.m. /f.* – miser, greedy person (*lit.* coin-sucker)

Sucette *n.f.* – hickey, red mark left on the skin from a kiss

Suçon *n.m.* – lollipop

Sucrer *v., Fr.* – to sugar, to sweeten
  ✱ *se sucrer le bec* – to eat, particularly sweets

Suisse *n.m.* – squirrel

Suiveux *adj., n.m. /fem.* – follower (not a leader)

Supporter *v.t.* – 1. *Fr.* to put up with; 2. to encourage, to support

Supposé(e) *adj.* – supposed (to)
  Elle est supposée y aller. – She's supposed to go (there).
  ✱ *être supposé de* – to be supposed to

Supposément *adv.* – supposedly

Sur *prep., Fr.* – on
  ✱ *être sur le bord de* – to be about to

Surprendre *v.* – to surprise
  Ça me surprend un peu. – That surprises me a bit.

Swell *adj.* – well-dressed, chic

Swinger *v.i.* – to party, to dance, to have a good time
  Ça va swinger ce soir. – It's gonna be a blast this evening.
  ✱ *ça swing en grand* – to work beautifully

Swing la bacaisse dans l'fond de la boîte à bois *expr.* – traditional square-dancing expression, used to poke fun at more portly female dancers (*lit.* swing your backside at the bottom of the buffet [table])

Switcher *v.* – to change, to switch

Système de son *n.m.* – sound system, stereo

T

Tabagie *n.f.* – newspaper stand

Tabarnac *expl.* – goddamn (*lit.* the tabernacle, where the Eucharist is kept in a Roman Catholic church)

Table à café *n.f.* – coffee table

Table d'hôte *n.m.* – restaurant's daily special, usually including an appetizer, a main dish, and dessert and/or coffee (*lit.* host's table)

Tablette *adj.* – room temperature
Cette bière est pas mal tablette! – This beer is pretty much room temperature!

Taboire *expl., def.* *"tabarnac"* – hell
C'est une taboire de belle opportunité. – It's one hell of a great opportunity.

Tag ou bitche? *expr.* – Heads or tails?

T'à l'heure *expr., def.* *"tout à l'heure"* – 1. earlier; 2. later

Tannant(e) *adj.* – boring, annoying
L'histoire était un peu tannante. – The story was a bit boring.

Tanné(e) (de) *adj.* – tired of, fed up, bored with (something/someone)
Viens-t'en, chérie, je suis tanné. – C'mon, sweetie, I'm tired of this.

Tanner *v.t.* – to bore, to make (someone) tired of (something)

Tantôt *adv.* – 1. before; 2. soon, afterwards; can be used in either sense, depending on the context or the tense of the verb it's used with.
Je t'appellerai tantôt. – I'll call you later.
Tantôt tu m'avais dit que non. – Earlier, you (had) told me no.
✶ *À tantôt!* – See you later!

Tant que *Fr.* – as for
✶ *tant qu'à y être* – insofar as that may be (the case)

Taoin *n.m.* – simpleton, imbecile

Taper *v.t., Fr.* – to tap, to smack, to hit
- ✳ *se taper une broue* – to have a beer
- ✳ *taper sur les nerfs* – to exasperate, to annoy (*lit.* to hit on one's nerves)

Il arrêtait pas de me taper sur les nerfs. – He wouldn't stop annoying me.

Tapette *n.m.* – effeminate man

Tapis *n.m., Fr.* – carpet, rug
- ✳ *mettre la musique dans le tapis* – to play music at high volume (*lit.* to put music in the carpet)

Taponnage *n.m.* – hesitation, dallying

Taponner *v.i.* – to dally, to beat around the bush

Arrête de taponner et donne-moi la réponse! – Stop dallying and give me the answer!

Taponneux(euse) *n.m./fem., adj.* – one who hesitates or dallies

Tarla *n.m.* – idiot, fool

Tas *n.m.* – a bunch, a cluster (of something)

Tata(aise) *n.m./fem., adj.* – 1. goodbye wave; 2. imbecile, simpleton
- ✳ *faire tata* – to wave goodbye

Tataouinage *n.m.* – indecision, hesitation

Tataouiner *v.i.* – to fool around, to waste time (on unimportant things)

Tax de Bienvenue *n.m.* – Welcome Tax; typically taxes owed to the Quebec Government upon purchase of a new home.

Teigne *n.m./fem.* – pestering or harrassing person

Téléphone *n.m.* – 1. *Fr.* telephone; 2. telephone call

J'ai eu un téléphone de lui hier. – I got a call from him yesterday.

Téléroman *n.m.* – TV series, such as a sitcom or soap opera

Tempête de neige *n.f.* – snowstorm

Temps *n.m., Fr.* – time
> ✱ *à temps* – in time
> *Ne t'inquiète pas, il va arriver à temps.* – Don't worry, he'll arrive on time.
>> ✱ *avoir le temps dans sa poche* – to take one's time, to go slowly (*lit.* to have the time in one's pocket)
>> ✱ *faire du temps* – to do time (in prison)
>> ✱ *temps des sucres* – the period during which maple syrup is harvested (typically March through April) and sugar shacks (*cabanes à sucre*) are open.

Tends *v., def. "attends"* – wait
> *Tends minute!* – Wait a sec!

Tenir *v.t., Fr.* – to hold
>> ✱ *tenir à (quelqu'un)* – to care about (someone)
>> ✱ *tenir le gros bout du bâton* – to have the advantage (*lit.* to hold the big end of the stick)
>> ✱ *Je tiens beaucoup à toi.* – I care about you a lot.

Tenter *v.i., Fr.* – 1. to try, to attempt; 2. to tempt, to interest
> *Est-ce que ça te tente de venir avec nous?* – Are you interested in coming with us?
> *J'ai tenté de le faire tantôt.* – I tried to do it earlier.

Terre *n.f., Fr.* – earth
> ✱ *à terre* – exhausted, finished, dead
> *La batterie dans ma voiture est complètement à terre.* – My car battery is completely dead.
>> ✱ *(avec les) culottes à terre* – (with one's) pants down
>> ✱ *avoir la face à terre* – to be annoyed, to be vexed
>> ✱ *avoir la langue à terre* – 1. to be exhausted; 2. to be very hungry (*lit.* to have one's tongue on the ground)

Tête *n.f., Fr.* – head
- ✳ *avoir la tête à Papineau* – to be very intelligent
- ✳ *tête de rubber* – numskull, dunce (*lit.* rubber head)

Téter *v.i.* – to hesitate

Téteux(euse) *n.m./fem., adj.* – 1. bootlicker, brown-noser; 2. hesitant person

'Ti *adj., def.* *"petit"* – small
Je prendrais bien un 'ti café. – I'll take a small coffee.

Tieindre *v.* – to hold

Tiguidou *expr.* – okey-dokey

Tinker *v.t.* – 1. to fail, to tank, to go belly up; 2. to fill up (a car's tank)
Son projet va sûrement tinker. – His project is definitely going to fail.
Je vais aller tinker d'abord. – I'm going to fill up my car first.

Tipper *v.t.* – to tip (someone)

Tire (d'érable) *n.m.* – hot maple sirup spread onto snow to cool and wrapped around a stick to form a lollipop, which is a typical dessert made at a *cabane à sucre.*

Tirer *v.t., Fr.* – to pull
- ✳ *tirer la pipe à* – to pull someone's leg (*lit.* to pull the pipe)
- ✳ *tirer le diable par la queue* – to be very poor (*lit.* to pull the devil by the tail)
- ✳ *(se) tirer une bûche* – to join in a conversation, etc. (*lit.* to pull up a log)

Tizoune *n.m./fem.* – dunce

Toast *n.m.* – toast
- ✳ *aller aux toasts* – to score, to hit a goal

Toast doré *n.m.* – french toast

Toasté(e) *adj.* – 1. toasted, grilled; 2. drunk
  ✱ *toasté des deux bords* – completely sloshed, very drunk (*lit.* toasted on both sides)

Toaster *v.t.* – 1. to toast; 2. to overuse, to burn out

Toffer *v.t.* – to put up with (something), to tough (something) out
  Ça fait mal, mais je peux le tougher. – It hurts, but I can take it.

Tôle *adj.* – broke, penniless

Tolérer *v.i.* – to tolerate, to put up with someone or something

Tomate *n.f., Fr.* – tomato
  ✱ *recevoir quelque chose sur la tomate* – to be hit by something unexpected (*sim.* to catch it on the chin; *lit.* to catch something on the tomato)

Tomber *v.i., Fr.* – to fall
  ✱ *tomber en amour* – to fall in love
  ✱ *tomber en compote* – to fall to pieces
  ✱ *tomber sur les nerfs* – to exasperate, to annoy (*lit.* to hit on one's nerves)
  Il arrêtait pas de me tomber sur les nerfs. – He wouldn't stop annoying me.

Toppe *n.f.* – cigarette

Toquant(e) *adj.* – heavy, filling (for food)
  La bouffe était bonne et assez toquante! – The food was great and pretty filling.

Torcher *v.i.* – 1. to move rapidly; 2. to clean in a rough manner
  Y torche, ton char! – Hey, your car really moves!
  ✱ *s'en torcher** – to not care
  Je m'en torche s'il vient ou non. – I don't give a damn if he comes along or not.

Torchon *n.m.* – rag
- ✱ *À chaque guenille son torchon.* – To every girl her guy (*lit.* To each cloth its rag).

Tordre *v.t., Fr.* – to twist
- ✱ *tordre le bras (de quelqu'un)* – to twist (someone's) arm, to insist

Torrieux *expl.* – damn

Torvis *expl.* – damn

Toton *n.m., adj.m.* – idiot, fool

Totons *n.m. pl.* – boobs, breasts

Touche *n.f.* – drag, hit (of a cigarette, etc.)
- ✱ *prendre une touche* – to take a drag

Toué *exp., def.* "*tous les*" – all the
- ✱ *en toué cas* – in all cases

Touffe★★ *n.f.* – 1. woman of questionable reputation; 2. woman's genital hair

Toune *n.f.* – tune, melody

Tourlou *expr.* – toodleoo, used as goodbye

Tourmaline★★ *n.f.* – 1. woman's hat, usually of large proportions; 2. cow dung

Tourner *v.i., Fr.* – to turn
- ✱ *tourner dans le beurre* – to go nowhere (*lit.* to turn in butter)

Tourtière *n.f.* – meat pie

Tout(e) *n.m., Fr.* – all, everything
- ✱ *tout le kit* – everything, the whole bit
  On sort ensemble. On se voit deux, trois fois par semaine, tout le kit. – We're going out together. We see each other two, three times a week, the whole bit.
- ✱ *tout le long* – the entire time

Tout croche *adj., adv.* – 1. bad, badly; 2. dirty, distasteful
Tu parles espagnol tout croche. – You speak Spanish badly.

Toutoune *n.f., adj.* – small overweight woman, roly-poly woman

TPS *n.m.* – federal sales tax

Track *n.m.* – (train) track
* ✶ *être à coté de la track* – to be in error, to make a mistake (*lit.* to be next to the [train] track)
* ✶ *perdre la track* – to go nuts, to lose one's head (*lit.* to lose the track)

Traduisible *adj.* – able to be translated

Traîner *v., Fr.* – to drag, to haul, to tow
* ✶ *se traîner les pieds* – to drag one's feet, to take one's time

Traîne sauvage *n.m.* – sled, toboggan

Traîneux(euse) *n.m./fem., adj.* – 1. slow person; 2. someone who constantly makes a mess (leaving a trail of disorder)

Trâlée *n.f.* – procession, large quantity of things or people
Elle est arrivée à l'école avec sa trâlée d'étudiants. – She came to the school with her procession of students.

Tranquillement (pas vite) *expr.* – slowly, gently

Trappe *n.f.* – trap, mouth, yap
Ferme donc ta trappe! – Shut your mouth, already!

Traversier *n.m.* – ferry, water shuttle

Trente-sous *n.m.* – quarter, 25-cent piece (*lit.* thirty cents)

Trimer *v.t.* – to trim, to cut

Trippant(e) *adj.* – impressive, amazing, exciting

Tripper *v.t.* – 1. to dig something, to find something cool, to really like something; 2. to have a crush on (someone)
Je trippe sur son projet! – I really dig his project!

Trippeux(euse) *n. m./f., adj* – one who really enjoys something

Trognon *n.m.* – troll

Trôler *v.* – to troll, to try to catch someone or something

Il a pas arrêté de trôler pour un date toute la soirée. – He kept looking for a date the entire evening.

Trône *n.m.* – throne, toilet

✱ *être sur le trône* – to be on the throne

Trou *n.m.* – 1. *Fr.* hole. 2. a dive, a less-than-nice place

Va pas à ce bar-là. C'est un trou. – Don't go to that bar. It's a hole.

✱ *avoir le trou de cul en dessous du bras* – to be exhausted (*lit.* to have one's asshole under the arm)

✱ *boire comme un trou* – to drink like a fish (*lit.* to drink like a hole)

✱ *être dans le trou* – to be in trouble (*lit.* to be in the hole)

✱ *péter plus haut que le trou*★★ – to be a snob (*lit.* to fart above the hole)

✱ *trou de cul*★★ *(Fr.)* – asshole

Trouble *n.m.* – trouble, problem

✱ *Il n'y a pas de trouble!* – No problem!

Trou de beigne *n.m.* – doughnut hole

Truste *v.t.* – to have confidence in, to trust

T'sais *expr., def. "tu sais"* – y'know

Tuile *n.f.* – tile

Tuque *n.f.* – winter hat

✱ *attacher ta tuque (avec de la broche)* – to hang onto your hat, to be ready for something

Attache ta tuque, on va aller skier sur la piste difficile après! – Hang onto your hat, we're going to ski down the difficiult slope next!

Turluter *v.* – to hum, to sing

Tuyeau *n.m.* – 1. *Fr.* pipe; 2. connection (between people), an "in"

Twit *n.m. /fem., adj.* – idiot, fool, twit
   C'est un beau twit! – He's a complete idiot!

U, V

Ustensiles *n.m. pl., Fr.* – utensils, cutlery

Vacances de le construction *n.m. pl.* – yearly holiday for most of the construction workers in Quebec, typically during the second half of July.

Vache *n.f., Fr.* – cow
> ✱ *Le diable est aux vaches.* – used to describe a chaotic situation (*lit.* the devil is with the cows)

Vacher *v.i.*- to laze around, to loaf

Vaisseau *n.m.* – (big) cook pot

Valeur *n.f., Fr.* – value
> ✱ *être d'valeur* – to be a shame, to be unfortunate
> *C'est d'valeur, mais on est déjà pris.* – Unfortunately, we're already busy.

Valise *n.m.* – 1. *Fr.* suitcase; 2. trunk (of a car)

Varger *v.t.* – to beat, to strike with force
> *C'est pas vargeux* – It's not very strong. It's not brilliant.
> *Il était tellement fâché qu'il a vargé dans le mur.* – He was so angry that he hit the wall.

Vatendon *expr., def.* "*va t'en donc*" – go on then, you're kidding me

Vedg *adj.* – vegged-out, relaxed, at ease
> *Man, je suis complètement vedg.* – Man, I'm totally vegged out.

Vedger *v.i.* – to veg out, laze about, to loaf
> *Je n'ai rien fait toute la journée. J'ai vedgé sur le divan.* – I didn't to anything all day. Just vegged out on the sofa.

Veillée *n.f.* – evening
> ✱ *veillée au corps* – wake

Veiller *v.i.* – to spend the evening, usually at someone's house
On va veiller chez lui ce soir. – We're spending the evening at his place.

Veilleux(euse) *n.m./fem., adj.* – one who likes to go to bed very late

Vente *n.f., Fr.* – sale
- ✻ *vente de feu* – fire sale
- ✻ *vente de garage* – garage sale
- ✻ *vente de trottoir* – sidewalk sale

Venter *v.i.* – to be windy

Venteux(euse) *adj.* – windy

Ventiler *v.i.* – 1. to air out; 2. to blow off steam, to vent (one's anger)

Versatile *adj.* – multi-talented, skilled in several fields

Veston *n.m.* – suit jacket

Viande hachée *n.f.* – hamburger meat

Viarge★★ *expl., def. "Vierge"* – goddamit! (*lit.* Virgin, an allusion to the Virgin Mary)

Vidanges *n.f. pl.* – garbage, trash

Vidangeur *n.m.* – garbage man

Vider *v., Fr.* – to empty
- ✻ *vider le problématique* – to get to the bottom of the problem

Vignenne *n.m./f., adj.* – (one who is a) rascal, rebel

Virailler *v.i.* – 1. to circle, to circumnavigate; 2. to toss and turn in bed
On a viraillé dans le voisinage pendant une demi-heure, mais on n'a pas pu trouver sa maison. – We circled the neighborhood for half an hour, but we couldn't find his house.

Virer *v.i.* – to turn
- ✻ *aller virer à* – to head out to
- ✻ *virer de bord* – to turn around

✷ *virer fou* – to go nuts, to go out of one's mind

✷ *virer sur le top* – to become the best

Viser *v., Fr.* – to forsee, to predict
Je vise que ça pourrait prendre une bonne semaine. – I'd say it could take a good week.

Visionner *v.t.* – to watch (a film, etc.)

Visite *n.f.* – visitors
✷ *avoir de la visite* – to have house guests/company

Vitement *adv.* – quickly

Voir *v., Fr.* – to see
✷ *voir (quelqu'un) dans ma soupe* – to be caught up with someone, to be head over heels for someone (*lit.* to see [someone] in my soup)

Votation *n.f.* – voting

Vous autres *pron.* – y'all, you all

Voûte *n.f.* – vault, safety deposit box

Voyage *n.m.* – trip, voyage
✷ *avoir son voyage* – to have had enough, to be fed up
C'est la dernière fois que je passerais une soirée chez eux. J'ai mon voyage! – That's the last time I'll spend the evening at their place. I've had enough!

Voyons donc! *expr.* – C'mon! I don't belive it! (*lit.* let's see then)
Voyons donc! Je veux te voir. – C'mon! I want to see you.

Vues *n.f. pl.* – movies
✷ *aller aux vues* – to go to the movies
✷ *écouter une vue* – to watch a movie

W

Wack *n.m.* – shout, yell

- *lâcher un wack* – to let out a yell

Watcher *v.t.* – to oversee, to keep an eye on (something/someone)

Wôw (là) *interj.* – stop, that's enough

X, Y

Yâble *n.m., def.* *"diable"* – devil
- *sentir l'yâble* – to smell awful (*lit.* to smell like the devil)

Y'a ça *expr., contr.* *"il y a ça"* – there is that (i.e., that is true)

Y'a rien là *expr., contr.* *"il n'y a rien là"* – it's unimportant, there's no issue

Yeule *n.f., def.* *"gueule"* – mouth

Yeux *n.m. pl, Fr.* – eyes
- *avoir des yeux dans la graisse de bines* – to be glassy-eyed (*lit.* to have one's eyes in the bean grease)
- *avoir des yeux pochés* – to have rings around one's eyes
- *avoir des yeux ronds comme des piastres* – to have eyes round like saucers
- *avoir des yeux (tout) croches* – to have squinty eyes
- *avoir des yeux tout le tour de la tête* – to have eyes in the back of one's head
- *avoir les deux yeux dans le même trou* – to be exhausted, to be staring at a point in space (*lit.* to have both eyes in the same hole)
- *coûter les yeux de la tête* – to cost a fortune (*lit.* to cost the eyes from your head)

Yinque *expr., def.* *"il n'y a que"* – only

Z

Zarzaille *adj.* – idiotic, foolish

Zézine★ *n.f.* – penis

Zigner *see* Zigonner

Zigonnage *n.m.* – fooling around, stupidity

Zigonner *v.i.* – 1. to attempt without much success; 2. to fool around, to waste one's time

Zigoune *n.f.* – cigarette (butt)

Zipper *n.m.* – zipper

Zipper *v.t.* – to zip (up)
   Il faudrait zipper ton manteau. – You'd better zip up your jacket.

Zozo *adj.* – idiotic, foolish

Conclusions

The past few hundred pages of this book clarified in black and white the vocabulary that anyone who understands basic French needs to acquire in order to speak and understand the language used in and around Quebec.

This book has explained the most important – and several of the most confusing – words and phrases heard in day-to-day Québécois speech. From initial grammar differences and slang through the swears and *jurons* to the lexicon, this book has already proven to be a reliable reference for countless visitors to and residents of Quebec.

From a language and accents perspective, this book largely reflects the Montreal area. Quebec is, of course, an enormous province, and so it goes without saying that there are many, many regional expressions and accents that are beyond the scope of this book and that may be discovered by the reader when travelling around the province.

This fourth edition is most certainly not the last. While this work already contains the most important set of everyday words you will hear in the province, the language is constantly evolving, and the total number of "unique" words in Quebec is actually somewhere north of ten thousand.

Thank you again for reading this work. I hope it provides you with a useful tool and becomes a handy pocket-book that allows you to gain access to the amazing richness and creativity that is *la province du Québec*.

References

Armange, Claire. *Parlez-vous québécois?* {Saint-Sébastien-sur-Loire, France}: Éditions d'Orbestier, 2007.

Bélanger, Mario. *Petit guide du parler québécois.* {Montréal, Canada}: Les Éditions Internationales Alain Stanké, 1997.

Béliveau, Marcel. *Savoureuses Expressions Québécoises.* {Monaco}: Éditions du Rocher, 2000.

Bergeron, Léandre. *Dictionnaire de la langue québécoise.* {Montréal, Canada}: Typo, 1997.

Bertrand, Guy. *400 capsules linguistiques.* {Montréal}: Lanctôt Éditeur, 1999.

Corbeil, Pierre. *Le québécois… pour mieux voyager.* {Montréal, Canada}: Éditions Ulysse, 1999.

Côté, Jean. *Expressions populaires québécoises.* {Montréal, Canada}: Quebecor, 1995.

Denoeu, François. *French Idioms.* {Hauppage, New York, USA}: Barron's Educational Series, 1996.

DesRuisseaux, Pierre. *Dictionnaire des expressions québécoises.* {Montréal, Canada}: Hurtubise HMH, 1990.

DesRuisseaux, Pierre. *Dictionnaire des proverbes québécois.* {St. Laurent, Canada}: Typo, 1997.

DesRuisseaux, Pierre. *Trésor des expressions populaires.* {PLACE}: Fides, 1998.

Dubé, Gilberte. *Dictionnaire des expressions imagées.* {PLACE}: Les Éditions Internationales Alain Stanké, 1998.

Dugas, André, and Bernard Soucy. *Le dictionnaire pratique des expressions québécoises.* {PLACE}: Logiques, 2000.

Dulude, Yvon. *Dictionnaire des injures québécoises.* {Montréal, Canada}: Les Éditions Internationales Alain Stanké, 1996.

Durand, Marc. *Histoire du Québec.* {Paris, France}: Imago, 1999.

Forest, Jean. *Anatomie du parler québécois.* {Montréal, Canada}: Triptyque, 1996.

Gazaille, Marie-Pierre. *Le parler québécois pour les nuls.* {Paris, France}: Éditions First, 2009.

Gaborieau, Antoine. *La langue de chez nous.* {Winnipeg, Canada}: Éditions des Plaines, 1999.

Guévin, Marie-Lou. *Les 1000 mots indispensables en québécois.* {Paris, France}: First Editions, 2011.

Gouvernement du Québec. *Le français au Québec.* {Québec, Canada}: Conseil de la langue française, 2000.

Keith-Ryan, Heather. *Quebec: bonjour, eh?.* {Bedford, Canada}: Sheltus & Picard, Inc. & VOA Publications, 1998.

Mansion, J. E. *Heath's Standard French and English Dictionary.* {Boston, USA}: DC Heath & Company, 1939.

Meney, Lionel. *Dictionnaire québécois français.* {Montreal, Canada}: Guérin Éditeur, 1999.

Proteau, Lorenzo. *Le français populaire au Québec et au Canada.* {Boucherville, Canada}: Les Publications Proteau, 1991.

Proteau, Lorenzo. *La parlure québécoise.* {Boucherville, Canada}: Les Éditions des Amitiés Franco-québécoises, 1996.

Scheunemann, Britta. *Le québécois de poche.* {Chennevières-sur-Marne, France}: Assimil, 1998.

Simard, Josée. *Comprendre le parler québécois.* {Paris, France}: Édimag, 2012

Tétu de Labsade, Françoise. *Le Québec un pays une culture.* {Montrea, Canada}: Boréal, 1990.

Online Sources

Lexique Québécois

http://www.angelfire.com/pq/lexique/lexique.html

"Quebec French Profanity," Wikipedia

http://en.wikipedia.org/wiki/Quebec_French_profanity